JESUS
IN MY LIFE

Sylvie Sauvé

Alexandria, Ontario, Canada

CLAY BRIDGES
PRESS

*"I came to bring fire to the earth,
and how I wish it were already kindled!"*
(LUKE 12:49 NRSV)

Contents

Introduction 1

Chapter 1: A Choice of Life 3

Chapter 2: Luke, A Triggering Element 15

Chapter 3: My Spiritual Awakening 23

Chapter 4: Mark, A Reliable Witness 33

Chapter 5: Health 43

Chapter 6: New Age 45

Chapter 7: The Relationship 61

Chapter 8: The School 69

Chapter 9: Blessings Received 79

Chapter 10: Unexpected Illness 83

Conclusion 91

Introduction

One morning, I received a revelation while I was going about my usual daily routine. I heard a voice asking me to write about my testimony. That same voice revealed the name of the book was to be "Jesus in My Life." The Holy Spirit, the source of this voice, explained that the title was special because it was intended to help everyone, as Jesus is in everyone's life.

Since my childhood, my profound desire has been to help all humanity. After a long journey, Jesus showed me the way, and it is with joy that I share my experience to help you through your own life journey.

You will find many answers to existential questions and a lot of clarification on faith. It should be noted that I am not bringing anything new to the Christian faith. What changed in my life is that I took the teachings in the Bible seriously. Going to church was no longer just an option but a river of life waiting for me.

The Lord always guides us safely, for He is "[. . .] the way, and the truth, and the life." (John 14: 6 NRSV). My hope is that after reading this book, you will be encouraged to make better life choices, and, as a result, the Lord will be able to bless you and protect you. I have searched so long for the truth! When we understand who we are in Him, it makes life all the more pleasant. I hope this book will also allow you to live a beautiful intimacy with Jesus, who wants to fill you with His joy and peace.

Lord Jesus, I give you all the readers in Your hands. May the Holy Spirit enlighten all Your children. Give them the blessings they need to understand their lives better. May they feel Your presence and Your Love all the time, everywhere, and under all circumstances.

CHAPTER 1

A Choice of Life

As a child, I recall vividly hearing a teacher in a schoolyard saying from far away, "Line up, children! Align in one row." Seeing the students line up, I did the same. Not knowing where I was going, I placed my trust in an unknown future. It was no use asking myself questions. Since I was only eight years old, I figured I had time to see where this path would lead me.

I was born in Vaudreuil-Dorion, Quebec, Canada, where I lived with my parents and my sister. My parents built their house on an abandoned lot, which they later discovered was the site of what began as a chapel and was later recognized as the Holy Trinity Church. The first Mass took place on July 3, 1896. When my parents bought the lot, the church was no longer housed there because the building had fallen into disrepair.

I attended school in that town. Throughout my elementary school years, I struggled with reading and writing. The teachers did not teach literacy, and they barely wrote on the blackboard. We didn't even have manuals! It was as though they were assuming the students knew the material beforehand. I had a hard time making any progress.

There were no specific subjects taught, and nothing seemed clear to me. I was unable to take notes on any topic, and my grades were poor. One day, just before the end of the school year, my mother received a call saying I had failed third grade. The school suggested that I go to summer school to catch up on my studies. By taking these courses, I had a chance to pass for the year. I accepted the offer and decided to go to summer school, but it was not easy.

I had to go to school every morning while watching other kids playing outside and having a good time. At the beginning of each class, an instructor gave out photocopies. I had to answer all kinds of questions. There was a different pile every day. I tried my best to answer all the questions properly. Even in summer classes, no one taught. All I had to do was answer questions and give those documents back to the monitor before I left. The same happened week after week. I was disappointed because they didn't even give me feedback on my work.

By the end of summer school, they still wouldn't let me move on to fourth grade. I had to start the third grade all over again; however, this time, something was different. My grades were excellent. I didn't understand why because their teaching methods hadn't changed, and yet I still had A's. I didn't say anything. I kept doing my best every day. I got through the year without any problems.

I will always remember the first day I started grade four in public school. Just before entering class, all the students were waiting in line to go into the school. The teacher was going up and down the line inspecting each child. When she finally reached me, she said, "You will not succeed in your year."

I didn't say a word; I was so shocked I couldn't speak. Regardless of her comment, I tried my best to succeed. Contrary to the previous year, my grades were now barely passing. No matter how hard I worked, my grades did not reflect my effort. I still didn't have any books or documents to learn from. We were expected to know the material ahead of time. I didn't know what more I could do.

During the year, we occasionally had a substitute teacher. When that happened, the day wasn't the same. It was always pleasant, and I was familiar with the answers. Yet when the permanent professor came back, it was like before.

The end of the year was quickly approaching, which meant final examinations were about to begin. I kept diligently working and doing my best. When the first day of the exams started, I was surprised! It was the substitute teacher. She briefly explained that the permanent professor had become ill. She couldn't show up at school to hand out the tests.

Little did I know that during this time, my parents were trying to transfer me to another school. They could see that the school was not going to give me a bright future. My mother kept saying, "Do your best on the tests." I tried my hardest to be successful; I was thinking positively daily. I wanted to please my parents. I knew I could do it, and I was trying hard.

Soon afterward, I received my scores. They were all passing grades. I was so relieved! I gave the test results to my mother with a smile. She was very happy. This was the moment my mother announced the possibility of me switching schools.

Just before the end of my school year, we had an appointment with the principal of the new school. The meeting took place in his office with my parents present. Then I had to talk to him in private. I was very shy. He asked me to read a text. I had some difficulties, but I did my best. My parents were brought back into the principal's office, and this time, I had to wait in the hallway. I was pacing up and down nervously. I could see the students in class with their teacher. The time seemed to stand still because I wasn't sure what to expect.

After my parents left the director's office, we drove home. While we were on the road, my parents announced that I was officially accepted into this new, privately-run school. This was fantastic news! I was so happy. The principal told my parents that the teaching method used by the public schools came from France. They assumed that once the child saw the beginning of a word, the student would automatically know the rest. That particular program failed in France, but the Quebec system wanted to test it. I was relieved because someone in the education system was aware of what was happening. I finally felt understood, and it felt great! The principal suggested that I should read more during the summer. He explained their school was more advanced than the government's curriculum, which meant I had to be ready to work hard. He accepted me in fifth grade and felt I could succeed. I was delighted with this change and ready for the challenge.

Both my parents and I had to make sacrifices to make this possible. Because it was a private school, my school fees were expensive. For my part, I had to give up ballet lessons, which I liked. I also had to travel a lot further, and the expectations were higher. My confidence level was low, but I didn't let that discourage me.

The following year, my mother, who was working for my previous school as a midday guardian, talked to the fourth-grade teacher, saying that I had succeeded in my year. She answered my mother by saying if she had corrected my tests, I would have failed. This confirmed she had wanted me to fail. She had her mind set the whole time. My confidence level was very low, but knowing this was done with such malicious intent proved I didn't have a learning disability. This changed my perspective. I tried to stay motivated.

When I started attending private school, I was nervous. On my first day, I realized I had no friends. I didn't know anybody. I felt so empty. Soon I ran into my ballet teacher. She recognized me as I had been attending her school for a few years. While I was speaking with her, I started to cry. Quitting ballet school for a better education was difficult. This change was hard because I enjoyed dancing. While I was talking to her, it was as though I was trying to convince myself that my sacrifice was worth it.

I worked hard every day in that new school. It was different, but at least I was learning. I had several topics to learn. They were letting us take notes, and I had textbooks. Finally, the learning material was accessible. With a lot of perseverance, my grades rose along with my confidence. I was able to learn without any issues. The material taught was clear. They gave us tests every week. I knew the material because they explained it, and I was now able to make progress.

Because my grades kept improving, my confidence soared, which helped me a lot. Instead of being a burden, learning became a great joy. My results brought me a lot of satisfaction. I could finally see that the work I was putting into my studies was showing. Now that I was fortunate to be able to learn, I wanted to know what other schools had to offer. I wanted to learn many more topics.

I felt like a lion out of its cage. I had been prevented from moving forward for far too long, and I was now free to learn and discover the world around me. Now that I was able to understand the material and succeed in my courses, I wanted to study as long as possible. It brought me great happiness and contentment.

Private school authorities encouraged their students to study and have as many degrees as possible. They talked about the labor market being competitive. We were told that having a university degree would improve our chances of moving forward in life. That explanation confirmed my resolve. I was focused on going to university; my goal was set.

At this time in my life, I had faith in God. My parents and I went to Mass every Sunday. I liked to sing the beautiful and meaningful songs to God from my bench. During the celebration, I tried to understand the readings. Sunday school wasn't available, so I learned what I could, as the homilies were difficult to comprehend. A child's perspective on life is not as advanced as that of an adult, but I always went to Sunday Mass out of respect for my parents and a desire to know more about Jesus. I loved God, and I wanted to please Him.

Early one morning, I heard a voice saying, "You will lose your faith to have a stronger one." At the time, I didn't realize the impact this revelation would have on my life. I didn't think this would affect my life in a negative way. Since I was able to learn, I didn't see any obstacles in my path. I attempted to understand faith and tried to make others happy. However, my main focus was obtaining a degree. In the end, I thought to myself that my faith wasn't a priority. I needed to focus on what I wanted to do with my life. As time went by, I looked at life with a lot of ambition. Things had to go my way.

My main preoccupation at the time was to complete my studies. I wanted to graduate from school and then go to college to further my studies. By the end of high school, I was forced to make my first big decision in life. Determining what you want to do with your life is an incredibly daunting task. Today, the list of careers is almost limitless, and my interest in a variety of subjects is constantly growing. It was difficult to decide. I was interested in law. Justice was important to me, so I applied to a program that would meet the university's requirements.

In Quebec, before entering university, students must complete at least two years of college. I submitted my application in humanities with an administrative profile. These courses allowed me to meet the demands of the university for law. Unfortunately, there was no specific legal training to prepare me for university, but since the program met the prerequisites, I was confident.

During my studies, I began to feel confused. I felt my education did not lead me to law school. The topics were broad, and they hardly made any references to law. I was introduced to history, politics, psychology, and mathematics. These were all interesting topics, but I didn't feel they were preparing me for the future I had planned. Everything was vague. It was not too late to change my mind at this point, and I began to reconsider my choice of career path. I thought perhaps I could still find a talent or even a passion to pursue, but that was not the case. Those two years allowed me to discover other subjects that fascinated me, which made choosing my career even harder.

In order to continue my education, I had to leave my family and live in Montreal. Because there was not enough space in the college residence, the administrator gave me the name of a nun who had rooms to rent. After a short visit, I agreed to the living arrangement. Since leaving my parent's house, I hadn't attended Mass. One Sunday, the nun who had rented me the room asked if I would like to go to church with her. I agreed.

The church was a short distance away. During the celebration, the readings and homilies remained unclear. I failed to understand the truth. While I looked at the people around me, I noticed they were a lot older. I felt like I didn't belong. I never went back to church with the nun. I simply didn't understand the Bible, God's plans, and faith.

One day, the nun asked if I wanted to visit her convent. I agreed. She wanted to see a sister who was ill. I went along with her. I respected the nun's values and beliefs. I never knew why she became a nun; I never asked about it. We took the bus, but there was no in-depth conversation. Upon arrival, I noticed the convent was quite big. There were many rooms. We spoke to the nun who needed comfort. I felt she was happy to see me and have company. After the visit, I went back to my room. We didn't talk any more about it.

During this time, I continued telling myself that what mattered was my career. Another semester was completed, and I passed all my courses with a good GPA, which was quite encouraging. However, I found myself disappointed. I was trying to find a talent. I wanted to specialize in something I could cling to and study forever. At the time, it seemed impossible to find since I loved so many different topics.

One day, the nun invited all the tenants to a meeting. Three other students were living there with me. Nobody knew what she wanted to talk to us about. When the time came, we all sat around the kitchen table. She lit a candle and placed it in the middle of the table, and started talking to us about our faith in Jesus. The reaction was remarkable! The students were shocked, and some were even insulted. Within a few weeks of this event, two tenants moved out. For my part, I stayed only because I didn't have any choice. The college residence still didn't have any rooms available.

As time passed, I faced a life filled with uncertainties. On the one hand, I heard a student who moved to the college residence criticizing the nun. On the other hand, I respected her religious beliefs. The nun opened her house to students, prayed, and visited the sick. There was something noble in this.

As the upheaval in the house settled back down, I was overwhelmed by the question: What do I do with my life? I didn't have any direction. I wanted to leave, but there was no good reason for me to do so. I just felt trapped. I didn't have my own identity, I had no experience, and I didn't stand for anything. The world wasn't clear. I simply followed what I thought was right and tried to be positive. I struggled with indecision.

The nun once asked me what I wanted to do in life. What a question! I told her I wanted to be an attorney. She replied, "Some of our nuns are lawyers." Her answer revealed her intention. I was not ready to become a nun. I was confused, but I had no intention of following that path. I wanted to work and be self-sufficient. I didn't know much about Jesus. I didn't understand the Bible. I didn't even know where to get information regarding my faith. The only thing I knew was Sunday Mass. I didn't know anything else about faith. Even after attending Mass each Sunday for so many years, I didn't feel anything different. I didn't even feel like I was maturing in that area. It just felt empty. I felt that faith didn't bring anything to my life.

The nun opened a door for me, but I closed it tightly and immediately. I was not ready. I wanted a career. I thought, "No, it's not possible." I can work for a living. I want to do as I please. I'm entitled to make my own decisions. Even if I was unsure about my future, I still didn't feel ready to face community life. I didn't know anything about it. I felt as though I was in front of a great abyss. Things were dark, with no clear future and no goal.

In those days, I had a boyfriend. We went to the same college. We met shortly before finishing high school. He was very talented and was always at the top of his class. He asked me to attend his high school graduation with him for our first date. It was an honor for me. During the evening, he won the Governor's Medal for his academic accomplishments. It was incredible!

At college, he studied a great deal of science. He wanted to be a physician. I admired his plan and his commitment. Needless to say, he was busy, and I respected that, so we didn't see much of each other. His schedule only allowed us to see each other every second Saturday.

Every weekend, I would go back to my parent's place to study. One weekend, when I came back to Montreal, the nun asked if my boyfriend was happy to see me. I found this question horrible. Why would he not be happy? We loved each other and made a lot of sacrifices for him to study. We would only allow ourselves to see each other twice a month. It was hard, but I respected his choice. I didn't want to be a burden. I wanted to give him the chance to succeed in his studies. I went to my room, furious and sad about the nun's question.

A few days later, the administrator of the college residence called to say there was a room available. What a relief! I moved out as soon as I had a chance. The influence of others, my uncertainties, and my lack of orientation led me to this choice.

Just when things couldn't be harder, my boyfriend wanted to meet me near the residence. This was unusual because he was always busy. I was surprised by our conversation. He wanted to end our relationship and stay friends. Since I loved him and we only saw each other twice a month, I already considered him a friend. I didn't want to see him again. Our relationship wasn't getting anywhere. When we met or spoke to each other, I felt I was wasting his time. I decided that it was better to stop seeing each other altogether. I wished him all the best in his future endeavors. I was sure he would succeed. It was difficult to move on, but I quickly recovered from that relationship.

Now, I had to face my future alone. My college program was about to end. I had to consider going to university. What area would I choose to study? I still didn't know, and time was running out. After so many years of studying, I found neither talent nor passion. How disappointing! Did I have a preference for one topic in particular? As much as I liked the idea of becoming an attorney, I didn't feel prepared. That's when another idea came to mind. I'll be an accountant! Since I was studying a lot in math, I felt better prepared in that field than in any other.

I tried to convince myself to take this direction even though math was very difficult for me. I met a friend while studying math. He was so kind. He would often explain some of the math lessons I was struggling with. That was such a blessing! After telling him about my career choice, he had a lot of doubts, and rightfully so. He was helping me so much to succeed! Without his help, I wouldn't have been able to pass all my math courses. I had to complete differential and integral calculus, stats, vector algebra, and linear geometry. These classes were required for both law and accounting programs.

Since I liked challenges, I decided to enroll in the accounting program. I encouraged myself by saying I could succeed in what I put my efforts into. The university accepted my application. Everything was set to move forward. At last, a clear path was now available to me. I was relieved and confident.

The summer before entering university, I worked as a receptionist in a hotel. It was near my parents' house. This experience helped me learn about life. I was happy to meet people from different countries, and it was nice to see vacationers having a good time. There is one thing I didn't like about the job. I had to charge people more for their rooms depending on the demand. This would embarrass me so much! Sometimes, there were only a few rooms available in the area. I found it hard to do, especially for families that came from far away. I wasn't well suited for that type of business. I started feeling bad about my career choice, but it was too late. My application was accepted.

Right from the start, nothing was going according to my plans for the upcoming school year. Before starting courses, I received a letter from the university requiring students to participate in a two-day seminar before classes began. At this seminar, the authorities strongly recommended the students change programs because there were already too many accountants in the workforce. After listening to two days of disheartening words, I was completely exhausted. Despite their advice, I decided to continue. I was motivated to work hard to succeed each semester.

At the start of classes in September, I realized that the program was not for me. The accounting professor explained the subject so quickly that it was difficult to understand. Despite my best efforts, I failed my accounting course. I passed all my other administrative courses but not accounting. What a deception! By failing this course, I had to reconsider my career choice. I asked to talk to a career counselor, but there were none available.

CHAPTER 2

Luke, A Triggering Element

One Halloween evening, I met Luke, a funny man in a suit. He was good at making people laugh. I appreciated his sense of humor. As I was talking to him, I admired his sense of direction. He wanted to work in cinematography. He had plans for filmmaking. It sounded interesting and so different from my own ambitions. I had no dreams to hold onto like Luke did.

We exchanged telephone numbers and left with no expectation of meeting again. I went on with my education. I was doing very well in my business classes, but I really needed to change my career path. The accounting courses were going too fast. They were not giving the students the chance to learn. Even the group average didn't pass. I was unsure what to do. What should I apply for? I started thinking about Luke and his cinematographic dreams.

One month later, I called him to see if he wanted to talk. He accepted. We went out to a bar and started talking. He liked to tell people about his plans, and I enjoyed listening. At one point in the conversation, he started telling me about a legal issue he was going through. He had planned to marry a woman named Isabelle, but his brother Jacques prevented him from doing so.

While they were engaged, Isabelle began to fall for Jacques instead of Luke. The wedding preparations had to end. Luke tried to talk to Isabelle. After speaking with her, she changed her mind and fell back into Luke's arms. When Isabelle talked to Jacques, he was furious. As a result of that discussion, they both showed up at the police station to file assault and rape charges against Luke.

When Luke found out what had happened, he went down to the police station to explain the story. Instead of clearing his name, the cops arrested Luke. Luke didn't understand. The cop told him that coming to the police station made him look guilty. Since Jacques and Isabelle filed criminal charges, Luke had to go to court and pay for a lawyer.

Because I had no direction in my life, I wanted to help Luke. He wanted to start his own company in cinematography. He had a lot of ambition, and I was willing to try to make his dreams a reality, no matter the challenges. A couple of weeks later, we moved into an apartment together. Being together, we had plenty of time to initiate the projects he had in mind. Even after many calls and all the different steps we took, we didn't get anywhere. Our lack of experience, training, and money forced us to look at things differently.

I found small contracts here and there as an administrative assistant. Without any experience or training in this field, it was not easy. I tried to find some kind of satisfaction in working even though I didn't like this type of job. Yet, I did enjoy helping people. When co-workers needed something, I tried to help as fast as I could. I also liked to make things easier for them.

Luke's ambitions continued to grow. He was never discouraged despite our lack of success. All my savings were spent trying to help him make movies. I was completely devoted to him and his dreams. I wanted to make sure his dreams became a reality. No matter what, it had to happen! Despite our best efforts, we still had no solid plans, no contract, and no direction.

My intention was to build a life with Luke, but I could see he had different plans in mind. As I talked to him about having a family, I was disappointed with his way of looking at life. He wasn't ready to commit himself to someone. Because of his experience with Isabelle, he didn't believe in love. According to him, I was there for a period of time, and that was it. He didn't want a long-lasting relationship. I was so hurt! I was there for him through thick and thin, and that was the appreciation I got after all the sacrifices I made to make him happy.

Meanwhile, his case was still underway. Our finances continued to shrink. We could no longer afford a lawyer, as the fees were so high! Luke had to defend himself without legal representation. We felt powerless.

One day, we received a call. It was Luke's brother, Jacques. He explained he had parted ways with Isabelle and wanted to withdraw his accusation against his brother. He wanted to try to bring the family together and correct his mistake.

Jacques did not want to go to court, but he was willing to write a letter stating the charges were false. So much frustration had occurred for no reason! We spent one afternoon typing a letter so Jacques could sign it as evidence that the charges were not true. We printed it, and it was signed by him.

Luke presented the letter to the court, but without an attorney, it didn't matter. The document was unofficial and seemed to be a fabrication. If Jacques had presented the story himself in court, he could have been charged for making up this story and wasting the government's money. The lawsuit had to go on anyway. After a few more appearances, the sentence was about to be pronounced. We were under a great deal of stress.

On the last day of the trial, the judge ruled. He convicted Luke on all accusations. I couldn't believe it. Many of his family members were there that day. They were saddened by the news, but Luke was devastated. My heart was shattered. From then on, I lost all faith in people and the justice system.

While Luke was incarcerated, I wanted to see him. This was very difficult, and I didn't know what to expect. I had never gone to a real jail before. When I saw him, we couldn't touch each other. There was a plastic wall between us. It was used to separate the visitors and the prisoners. There were phones that we could use to talk.

After that visit, I was really looking forward to seeing him back home. He had been sentenced to six months. Each month seemed like forever. I was looking forward to moving on with our lives. When he eventually got out, I noticed his personality had changed. We weren't as close as before. Luke became even more ambitious. He didn't want to waste any more time and decided to enroll us at the university. What a wonderful idea! I was a little disappointed because I was still unsure of what I was going to study, but I was sure I could find something.

I tried to think of a field, but I still didn't know what to choose, even after all my experiences. I got so caught up in Luke's situation that I lost touch with myself. This threw me off guard.

One evening, while I was painting our apartment, I stopped to look at all the programs available. There were so many to choose from. Suddenly, I came across language degrees. I found an undergraduate program in languages. Because I had a good knowledge of both French and English, I felt I could be successful in this field. I applied to that program, and a few months later, I received a letter saying I was accepted.

When school started, I was happy in this field. I finally felt like I belonged. I enjoyed all of my courses, and my grades were excellent. As for Luke, his studies no longer interested him. He was following a law course to help himself and others along the line. Luke got mad at the teacher. He couldn't accept the teacher saying justice was fair. After going through what he had, I understood how he felt. He decided to stop his studies and continued trying to find contracts in cinematography.

As for me, my education was becoming more and more interesting. I was motivated to finish my degree. I didn't want to be involved in his plans anymore. While I respected him and wanted him to continue on in cinematography, I no longer found the field interesting. Our lives started to shift in totally different directions.

Luke became increasingly preoccupied with his film projects. He discovered digital montage on computers, and it became a passion for him. He worked tirelessly to get contacts. It was great, but I was seeing him a lot less. He was hardly at the apartment.

When he was there, we didn't have as much in common as before. He was focused on his films, plans, and projects.

Determined to figure out my future, I realized it was better to leave Luke. Seeing as our views on family and career did not align, there was only one solution. It was time for me to move on. One day, when he showed up at the apartment, I spoke to him about it. His feelings were the same. I was relieved, but, at the same time, it was strange. We still loved each other, yet it was better to live our lives separately.

I moved to a smaller apartment. The landlords were friendly and looked after the welfare of their tenants. The solitude I encountered was difficult. I wasn't used to being alone. What was even more difficult, however, were all the existential questions that kept coming. Why did this relationship fail? We were together to love one another. My desire to help someone in need seemed like a good reason to build a lasting relationship.

To find the answers to all my questions, I decided to apply for free psychological consultations at the university. After at least ten sessions, I still had no support or direction. I shared all my existential questions, but I received no response, no answers, and no directions. At the end of each visit, I didn't feel I was moving forward. I was the only one doing the talking. The psychologist was just listening. I stopped the consultations knowing psychology couldn't help me.

Then one day, just before a health and fitness class began, a student asked me a favor. She was assisting the university's special needs office. She explained she wouldn't have time to tutor students next semester. She wanted to know if I would be interested in teaching someone who had special needs. I agreed straight away. The following morning, I went to the department. As I had an excellent average, they accepted my application. They said they would be in touch with me by the end of the semester.

A month later, I received a call from the department. They gave me Caroline's contact information. Since I had to help her with one of her courses, I had to sign up for the same course. The name of the course was Art Education for Children. Although this course was not part of my program, the university opened it for me. It was a great opportunity, and I was able to help a student while learning about early childhood education.

For the purpose of this class, I had to find a daycare that would allow me to work with children. It was difficult to find a daycare, but I was finally able to locate one nearby. Caroline and I didn't have access to the same daycare. I was sad about that because I was in that class for her, but she seemed to understand the situation. She needed help with the teachings and the readings. So that was fine. The purpose of this class was to observe children's drawings.

Once a week, I would go to the daycare and ask the children to make a drawing. I really didn't know where this task would lead me. I really didn't see much of a point to this, but I went along with the experience. The children responded quite well to the activity. As soon as I asked for a drawing, they would get to work. This was when I started to notice a difference. Not all children reacted the same way. Some children would draw each character very nicely with beautiful colors. Others would start their drawing with beautiful colors but then cover it with black. Others would draw aggressively using only black.

I didn't understand why certain children seemed more aggressive in their drawings than others. It was just a drawing. I could see their emotions being expressed through their drawing. The difference in their emotions was startling. These children were in the same daycare and with the same caretaker. What was causing the difference?

From week to week, I kept on asking them to do different drawings. We were always in the same room and in a relaxed atmosphere. The responses from the same children were consistent. It had nothing to do with the type of drawings or the location. While they were drawing, it suddenly became clear. At the end of the last art session, I wanted to talk about my observation to someone who knew the children. I was able to talk to the main caretaker about what I noticed.

I talked to her about my observations. I mentioned the children's reactions while they were drawing and the colors they were using. From there, I shared with her that it didn't have anything to do with the location and the caretaker, but it had to do with their family. More precisely, their art was linked to the marital status of their parents. The children who had divorced parents were expressing it in their art by using black. These children were more aggressive in their artwork. She confirmed the accuracy of my observation. I was shocked! The children were expressing the lack of love in their lives through their art. They were all under five years old. This class certainly opened my eyes as I discovered how important it is to love and be faithful to one another. Love, or the lack of it, creates a domino effect. It affects the people around us and us.

I continued my language classes at university with this experience in my heart. I decided to concentrate all my efforts on finishing my degree. With this goal in mind, I put aside all the emotional aspects of life. Upon completion of the program, I found I graduated with distinction. I felt joy as I graduated and expected a bright future ahead.

When I started working, I realized I still had a great deal to learn. In what? I didn't know exactly. With God's Providence, I was able to prosper. We rarely hear the word "providence" in our times, but it still exists. Providence means that God helps us to move forward. God guides our destiny. He has the power of sustaining us. He knows what we need to grow positively.

Not long after graduation, I found a full-time job. After a few years of work, I decided to enroll at another university to obtain a teaching permit in French and religion. Religion at that time had become a bit more important, but I still didn't have a clear direction. The books I read on the topic back then were vague. For the most part, I was reading New Age books.

This change in paths seemed to fill a need as opposed to securing professional advancement. Once I was at university, I lost interest in my studies. The religion teacher found it odd that I would drop out of the program since I had an A average. I realized that teaching others was an important responsibility, one I wasn't ready for. How could I teach spirituality when, in the end, I was the one who needed guidance? How could the blind lead the blind? I needed to end these studies. I needed to understand the true meaning of my life to begin with. But life seemed so vague and difficult to figure out.

CHAPTER 3

My Spiritual Awakening

moved in with my mother and father because I was unemployed. I was back in the workforce with a bigger set of questions. *How difficult life is*, I thought. *What is life all about? What does God want me to do in my life?* I felt like I was at the bottom of a barrel. Only then did I begin to look upward and think more about God.

In those days, God did not have a face. He was the Almighty and the Creator. I was struggling between the Christian faith and New Age. While I was lying in bed in my room with the shades down, I was thinking about my future. Suddenly, I had a vision. I saw a large hallway that led me to various classrooms. There were so many rooms! In one room, they taught meditation. In another room, they taught yoga. Now I knew what to do! I needed to learn more about spirituality!

I understood what this meant! I must help others spiritually. Although I did not have a great deal of knowledge in this field, I was ready to work hard to succeed. I was open to the experience. I read a few books on energy. At least it was a start. I looked through the local newspaper and found several classes in my area. I was sure that if I followed these teachings, I would finally be able to understand life, so I signed up for a lot of different subjects. I had a course every evening.

I was working full-time during the day. Right after work, I would have a quick dinner and attend classes with much interest. One night, it was yoga; another night, it was transcendental meditation, and so on. In other words, I was completely immersed in the New Age movement. I started learning about the power of crystals, chakras, channeling, tetrahedron, reflexology, yoga, transcendental meditation, horoscope, New Age Angels, tarot cards, pendulum, and clairvoyance.

The deeper I got into the New Age movement, the emptier I felt. I felt death in my heart. In a yoga class, the teacher asked us to turn around 50 times. After about 20 turns, I felt so dizzy physically, mentally, and spiritually. It was then that I decided to quit the yoga lessons and the New Age movement altogether. Taking a step back from what I learned over the past year, I realized each book has its own truth. New Age knowledge is not linked to other New Age teachings. There is nothing consistent between the different beliefs. Each author brings their visions and interpretations, but nothing comes out of them. It is empty. I was unable to get answers about life this way. I felt like there was no future in this movement for me anymore.

After realizing this, depression started to settle in. There was no light around me; everything was dark and lifeless. *What now?* What seemed to be God's path for me became a way to death. This was certainly not God's will. This thought, and many others, troubled me. All my unanswered questions kept coming to mind. *What is life? Why am I facing so many failures? Why didn't I have a good relationship? Why are some couples successful and others not? Who rules our lives? What is good? What is bad? Where can I learn more about life? What or who do I belong to? Is there a movement or an organization I belong to? Who am I?*

At that moment, I set myself a death goal. There was nothing left for me to live for. I was giving myself another year. If I couldn't find happiness during those twelve months, I would end my life. While I was sleeping one night, I had a dream. I saw the town I was living in. All the buildings and nature around me were black and white. Nothing was moving. It was lifeless. The only picture that had color was Jesus' face on a cross. This cross stood in front of the church in the town I was living in. This caught my attention, as the rest of the city was grey and dark, and unmoving. I woke up wondering what this dream meant.

Sometime later, after coming back from work, I asked myself this question, *What can I learn on Earth that will matter upon my death?* This added yet another question to my already long list of existential questions. This question, however, was the key I was looking for. If I could find the answer, I would get closer to the true meaning of life.

Later that day, I realized I felt empty. I couldn't continue living my life this way. I felt such a void. I didn't know what to do or where to get answers to all my questions. I didn't know where to go or who to talk to. I had tried it all, and yet, I still didn't have any answers. I was stuck. That's when I cried to Jesus in my heart. "Jesus, You came into this world to love, but I don't know how to love. I have searched for the meaning of life, but I am unable to find the answers. I want to hear it from the Source! I want to hear it from the Source! I want to hear it from the Source! I want to hear it from the Source!" After saying this last sentence at least ten times in my heart, I still felt empty. But, at the same time, I felt as though someone was listening.

From that point on, I lived one day at a time. I knew death was just around the corner. I couldn't go on living in confusion. I couldn't see myself having a boyfriend. How could I love another person if I couldn't love myself? What's the use of having children if I couldn't steer them in the right direction? I felt the walls of the barrel getting higher. I was now at the bottom of a large, narrow tower with big concrete blocks all around. The tower was round and extremely high. There was an opening on top of it. I could see the bright blue sky, but it was far above me!

On my quest to find answers to all of my questions, I found myself in Montreal at a used bookstore. I was hungry to learn about life, and I was hoping to find it in a book. During my research, I found a book titled *For the Happiness of My Own, My Chosen Ones—Jesus* (Volume 1) by Léandre Lachance. It sounded interesting, so I kept it and went about adding more books to my pile. When it was time to leave the store, however, I realized I had taken too many books for both my arms and my budget.

I had to sort all of them quickly because the store was about to close. When I came across the book *For the Happiness of My Own, My Chosen Ones—Jesus*, something told me to keep it. I listened to that little voice and paid for it.

When I got home, I placed all my newly purchased books in a bookcase. I didn't know which one to read first. My life was so difficult to bear; I needed hope. I felt a voice inside of me saying to start reading the book *For the Happiness of My Own, My Chosen Ones—Jesus*. Immediately after Christmas, I started reading it. The title seemed unreal for our times. I thought Jesus' chosen people were only for His apostles more than 2,000 years ago. Regardless, I decided to sit down and read the book.

After reading the first ten pages, my life changed. I realized the title was right. The book made me realize we are all disciples of Jesus even today. We are all His chosen ones.

What an amazing discovery! What was incomprehensible was now clear. I was blind, and Jesus gave me the possibility of seeing. I was deaf, and He made it possible for me to hear. What touched me the most in this book was reading the "I love you" from Jesus; how I needed to hear those gentle words! What a joy to know Jesus loves us and is near us! He is so close; He is within us! When I realized how intimate we are with God, I melted like snow under the sun.

Mr. Lachance was given private revelations by Jesus that were published in this book. Its message is for everyone. As I read, it was as though Jesus was speaking directly to me. I was under the impression He understood everything I was going through. I was so excited to read this book, and I began to feel relief and support. I was starting to find the answers I had been seeking for so long. As I was reading, I felt as though He wanted me to say *yes* to Him. Yes, I know You love me. Yes, I know that without You, I am nothing. Yes, I trust You, Lord. Yes, I want to submit to Your will, Lord. And yes, I want to abide by Your commandments. I was free to answer Him since God is Love. He doesn't make anybody follow Him, but deep down, I knew He was leading me to happiness. I knew He would help me understand life since He is Life. So, each day, I gave Him my yes.

Sometimes, following Jesus wasn't so simple. It often makes us think differently than the world expects us to. I wanted to stay with Jesus because I wanted to follow in His footsteps. I could feel how much He loved me. No one can love us that way, even with the best intentions in mind. It wasn't easy to realize the mistakes I had made in my life. All my sufferings came from saying "no" to Him and His commandments. The more I read, the more I kept on surrendering to Jesus. Each time I had a problem or felt happiness, I would give it all to Him right away.

At the time, I had just started a new job at a manufacturing company. There were many challenges to overcome. The whole company was re-organizing its procedures. Each task had to be done quickly and efficiently. For each assignment that was given to me, I would give it right away to Jesus. I had a big workload, but by giving it to Jesus, each task became lighter and even more enjoyable.

Jesus says in the Bible, "For my yoke is easy and my burden is light." (Matthew 11:30 NRSV). I realized it was true. Jesus' Word is dependable. I was beginning to understand that Jesus was my only hope, my only Master, and my Lord. My circumstances changed for the better. My supervisors were satisfied with my work. I knew it wasn't me, but it was the Lord who made it possible. The mountains before me were razed to the ground because I trusted Jesus. He gave me all the necessary blessings I needed to be happy at work and in my personal life. I finally found the answers to all my questions.

The more I read this book, the more I felt the need to repent of my sins. But how? For a Catholic, believers must confess to a priest. They taught confession at a young age. I vaguely remembered what the teacher explained when I was seven years old.

All I could remember was sitting down in front of a priest and talking about what I had done wrong.

In order to repent of my sins, I tried to find a church. On my way to work, I drove close to one each day. I decided to stop and look at the Mass schedule. I wanted to know when I could see a priest for confession. What joy! A Mass was held on Saturdays at 8 a.m. That was perfect! My plan was made.

I wrote down what my conscience was telling me, everything I regretted in my life. Due to a lack of education, I had no idea how to confess my sins. What are sins? What kind of prayers should I say before and after my confession? No one had explained this to me. I found a small book in my parents' library. This book gave me all the information I needed regarding confession. I wrote down the prayers to say first and last. The book also explained how to self-examine one's conscience. To make a good confession, we must see how we live according to God's Ten Commandments. The Bible mentions them twice, once in Exodus 20:2–17 and once more in Deuteronomy 5:6–21. I wrote all I had done against those laws of Love. I was ready to change my behavior and follow God's will from this moment forward.

At the end of my examination, I realized I had a lot to say. I could now clearly see all my failures, all my sins, and all my disobedience according to the Ten Commandments of God. I had only gone to an individual confession once. That took place at the end of the Sacrament of Penance course (also known as reconciliation or confession) course when I was just a child. I don't remember having the opportunity to see a priest privately since then. That meant I hadn't been to confession in over 20 years. I printed out my confession to God. I wanted to see a priest as soon as possible.

"When Gentiles, who do not possess the law, do instinctively what the law requires, these, though not having the law are a law to themselves. They show what the law requires is written on their hearts, to which their own conscience also bears witness, and their conflicting thoughts will accuse or perhaps excuse them on the day when, according to my gospel, God, through Jesus Christ, will judge the secret thoughts of all." (Romans 2:14–16 NRSV)

The following Saturday, I was prepared to ask Jesus for forgiveness for all my failings. I arrived ten minutes before Mass. Getting into the church wasn't as easy as usual. Knowing the burden of my sins, I struggled to enter the establishment. I was crying so much! I couldn't stop going in and out. How could I have made so many mistakes? My ignorance and my will had distanced me from God's Love. What made me so ignorant for so many years? My ignorance prevented me from being happy. I made so many bad decisions. Though the intent was love, the decisions were wrong. I had removed God from my life. I did not obey His Word. The Lord was waiting for me, but I turned my back on Him. It was so hard to walk into that church that day. My tears were out of hand, but my mind was made up. I had to do this. From that point forward, I wanted to follow Jesus. I wanted to repent. I decisively entered the church and attended Mass.

I sat on a pew at the back of the church. My heart started pounding so hard. During Mass, I thought about a lot of things. How could I have rejected God's Love? I rejected my Creator, my Saviour, and my Lord. I pushed away love, real Love. By putting God aside, I rejected myself. I chose unhappiness by being far from God. For so many years, I had suffered due to my own bad decisions and a lack of knowledge.

Throughout the celebration, my tears were running, and my heart was pounding. My heart was beating so quickly, it was difficult to bear. I was near a statue. It was the Sacred Heart of Jesus. I just had to talk to the priest! I couldn't delay this anymore. As soon as Mass ended, I went directly to the sacristy with a beating heart. With God's grace, the Lord gave me the strength to talk to the priest and ask if I could confess my sins. Three pages of regret were in my hands, and the priest greeted me as a father. He was patient and sympathetic. In the midst of my confession, I felt profound repentance and burst into tears.

With the encouragement of the priest, I ended my confession. After giving all my faults to the Lord, I received one of the Church's greatest gifts, absolution. At that very moment, Jesus forgave all my sins. I left the church and cried even harder, but I felt better. Despite my sorrow, I began to feel joy in my heart. By receiving God's forgiveness, Jesus could now help me move on because I was letting Him take over my life. I finally did the right thing. I was going by the rules.

During that week, I began to feel relieved. Shame and depression were already gone. These were great healings! Thank you, Jesus! Thanks to the Lord's mercy, I attended Mass the following Saturday. This time I decided to go to church well in advance. I arrived 30 minutes before mass. To my surprise, as I walked in, I found the priest was already in the confessional. I realized Jesus guided me to this church because of the priest's availability. How great this sign was in my eyes! It also meant I could come as many times as I wished. It is better to go to confession before Mass as a penitent. We must realize Whom we are receiving in Holy Communion. We must receive God with purity and sincerity. The most important thing for God is our soul, and it is our responsibility to listen to Him and say yes. I was now on the right path, thanks to God's mercy. I wanted to keep my soul clean and pure to receive my Lord, so I took advantage of the Sacrament of Penance as often as I could.

The church was not just a building to me anymore, but a place where we find the Lord's real presence in the Eucharist. What a difference this made in my life! God is close, and He gives us an abundance of life. How could I not enjoy Mass? How can we refuse to love the One who Loves us the most? The One who can make us happy?

God is in us; we can talk to Him, worship Him, praise Him, contemplate Him, thank Him, and entrust all our difficulties to Him anytime and anywhere. He is always there as a good friend and an awesome God. I even discovered that He is the One who waits for us and not the other way around. How great is God's Love! God is always available. He is never too busy to listen to us. If fact, He anxiously awaits us to talk to Him.

During my studies, I discovered another aspect of what friendship means. God wants us to love everyone; that is true. However, we must remain truthful. In 1 Corinthians 15:33 NRSV, the Bible says, "Do not be deceived: 'Bad company ruins good morals.'" This means we need to choose our friends wisely. It is fine to help those in need, but when it comes to sharing time with others, it is better to be with the people who will help you move positively through life and not encourage sin.

Pray for those who need help. You will still love them, and God can open their hearts. "Let no one deceive you with empty words, for because of these things the wrath of God comes on those who are disobedient. Therefore do not be associated with them. For once you were darkness, but now in the Lord you are light. Live as children of light—for the fruit of the light is found in all that is good and right and true." (Ephesians 5:6-9 NRSV)

CHAPTER 4

Mark, A Reliable Witness

Week after week, shame and guilt were lifted from my shoulders, my troubles were fewer, and my life was happier. After reading the book *For the Happiness of My Own, My Chosen Ones - Jesus*, I decided to read the Bible, which is the only book with all the answers. God gave us this book so we could make good decisions in all aspects of our lives.

All my existential questions have been answered because everything we need to know is in the Bible. At last, I found God's absolute peace! The Bible helps us because it is Truth itself. It is full of wisdom. Through God's mercy, I found a new life. I accepted the Truth, and I decided to make it my way of life. That's what Jesus meant when He said to Nicodemus, "[. . .] Very truly, I tell you, no one can see the kingdom of God without being born from above." (John 3:3 NRSV)

When we are born again or experience a conversion, this means the same thing, our perspective of life becomes profoundly rooted in Jesus and His Word. By saying *yes* to Jesus even in our sorrows, we are saying to God that we are willing to follow Him. When we say *yes* to Jesus, we say *yes* to God's Ten Commandments. There comes a time in every person's life when we start thinking more profoundly; we mature. We start thinking that there has to be something more to learn than what society is exposing to us. This world is filled with lies, and it will not bring the happiness we seek. The only One who can give us real joy and real peace is Jesus. "To set the mind on the flesh is death, but to set the mind on the Spirit is life and peace." (Roman 8:6 NRSV)

When we feel God's Love, we know He wants us to be happy. We come to realize that true happiness comes from within and not from events, people, or success. We are all God's children. Knowing that we can understand how much He values us. There are so many reasons to be thankful!

After this spiritual journey, I wanted to talk to the priest who was available for confession each Saturday morning. I made an appointment to thank him for being available for confession. I wanted to explain how important this was for me and for everyone. I also wanted to mention what had happened to me. As we spoke, the priest asked me if I knew Mark, who was also attending Mass each Saturday morning. Since I was new to the parish, I didn't know him. He explained that Mark was distributing the very book that converted me *For the Happiness of My Own, My Chosen Ones—Jesus*. There is no such thing as a coincidence. The Lord surely works in mysterious ways. I was happy for the opportunity to meet Mark so I could share my experience with him.

The following Saturday, Mark and I met for the first time. I spoke to him about the book that changed my life. It was a book he knew well, as it had also changed his life. After talking to him, he invited me to a restaurant along with his friends who attended Mass. I had a chance to continue to discuss my spiritual journey with Mark. I wanted to tell him about the blessings I received after reading this book. After telling him my story, he was not surprised. He experienced God's Love through that book as well. That was the reason he was distributing it. He was pleased to hear my testimony. It confirmed that the path of life is truly through Jesus Christ. No one could have made this change and given my life back except for God and His Word. What a joy it was to meet someone who understood me and was so devoted to God. It's as if God planned it all. It was simply incredible!

Every Saturday after church, I met Mark and his friends at the restaurant. They became my brothers and sisters in Jesus. We talked, laughed, and cried. We felt united because we could be true to each other. We were all following the same Master. I now had a group of friends I felt comfortable with. I could talk about Jesus, and they would understand. It was a wonderful feeling!

Many of them told me that confession helped them more than psychological counseling. I had to admit I felt the same way. It was the Sacrament of Penance that freed me and healed me of all sorts of evils. Over time, I realized that if it wasn't for Jesus, this could have been the day of my suicide. Jesus turned things around for the better. The pain of death I felt within me changed into life; a life led for Jesus.

Once a month, I made it a point to self-assess myself according to the Ten Commandments, and my entire being felt free. I finally had direction. I sensed I was in the grace of God, sheltered and surrounded by the Love of God. Life became clearer. I could now understand the reason for my misery and the world's issues. Sin, our lack of love and obedience to God, sets us apart from the source. God loves us so much that He cannot punish us. When we are miserable or unhealthy, we experience the consequences of our bad decisions and behavior. It is not God's fault, and it's not because God doesn't care. It's because we are not listening to Him and His teachings. He gave us everything we needed to be happy. We simply need to use all that He gave us. Yes, it works. Yes, He can protect us if we go according to God's Ten Commandments. Like a game, if we play by the rules, everything is predictable. We know where to go and what to do, and it's fun! When we don't follow the rules, everybody gets easily discouraged, and it's not fun.

Choosing not to repent and accept Jesus as Lord sets us against God. This is what we realize when we have a born-again experience. We are either for Him or against Him. There is no in-between. Our lives cannot function properly if we are going against our Creator. God created us; He knows what is best for us. It is important to listen to Him and be obedient to His Word. God is Love, and He is a good God. He wants what's best for us. He also wants us to be happy and successful. When we refuse His Love, we withdraw from God's blessings.

We often hear people saying that God does nothing in the face of disaster or war, but have we considered our behavior in each of these events? Jesus came to give us all the teachings we need to live in love and joy. It is our job to implement His teachings. If we fail to follow them, it is because we lack love for ourselves and others. We have to make the effort to love. It takes a lot of courage to follow Jesus. Nevertheless, we are never disappointed when we do. He rewards us all the time. If God asks you to give money, do it. Don't hesitate to give 10% of your income to the church you attend and can grow in. He will reward you for it. It is by living in faith that our intimacy with Jesus grows. No one can ever be disappointed when working with God.

After such a change in perception, I felt the need to withdraw for a week to think and pray. I found the Trinitarian House of Spirituality (Maison de Spiritualité des Trinitaires) in Granby, Quebec. I chose to live a week in silence. I felt comfortable being surrounded by religious people. I was pleased to be part of a group of people who shared the same beliefs.

While I was there, I realized all the wonders our forefathers left us. I was thinking about all the churches, shrines, and religious communities built in Quebec by people who put a lot of effort into the generations to come. Our ancestors left us the greatest legacy anyone could wish for: faith. Their commitment filled me with gratitude. They knew God was the priority in life. Their devotion to God is all around us, waiting for us to notice and appreciate it.

The Saints made history. They did what they could to give us better living conditions by building hospitals and schools. Their courage came directly from Jesus Christ. Despite their financial needs, labor, and the weather, their desire to help others was their main concern. It took a great deal of love, dedication, and patience to achieve so much, but they were successful with God's Providence.

At the Spiritual Center where I was staying, I was able to learn about the lives of several saints. The Saints gave us such positive examples. They lived according to the virtues: of humility, chastity, temperance, charity, diligence, patience, and kindness. Knowing the stories of people of faith is inspiring. Some saints, such as St. Therese of Lisieux, St. Augustine, St. Teresa of Avila, and St. Faustina Kowalska, wrote about their testimony. Others received revelations from Jesus Himself, such as St. Hildegard of Bingen and many others. They were able to love their brothers and sisters by prioritizing Jesus. Wonders still occur when we pray to the saints. They intercede on our behalf to Jesus to answer our prayers.

I remember some years ago, at the end of Mass, a man went to the podium of the church in tears. He wanted to testify to what St. Brother André had done on his behalf. He explained he was a truck driver who accidentally injured a child while backing up. In his great sorrow, this man prayed to Brother André for the healing of this child. Sometime later, the disabled child was miraculously healed. There were no more scars on the child's body. St. André interceded for him. His prayer was answered. It was a miracle! Thank you, Father, for your Love! How many other miracles have we encountered recently? The saints are there for us. We can ask them for help in our prayers, and they will intercede without fail on our behalf before God.

The shrine of Our Lady of the Cape in Trois-Rivières was built with the help of one such miracle. As the population kept increasing, they needed a bigger church. The small church was destroyed, and the rocks were kept to be used for the new construction. There were more rocks available on the other shore. Since the new church needed to be bigger than the previous one, those rocks on the opposite shore were needed for construction.

Winter was close to an end, and the river was starting to thaw. The workers couldn't get across the river to access the rocks there. Having prayed to Mother Mary and promised the church would be in Mother Mary's honor, the situation improved. The ice that was melting all jammed to make a path to the other side. The horses and the men could cross, get the rocks, and bring them to the building site. When the last load of rocks was transferred, the bridge of ice melted. Many witnesses saw this miracle and built a decorative Rosary Bridge to remember the heavenly help.

Along with learning about the saints, I continued to read my Bible and study. Each word in the Bible is a gift from God. Why should we feed off the words of men and women who have no guidance in their own lives? Most TV stations, newspapers, and magazines do not help us spiritually. They do not write by faith, but by what this world wants you to think. The media often steers us away from the true meaning of life. What is popular is often destructive. We must discern what the Lord wants us to do. God wants to protect us, but to be protected, we have to know Him and obey Him. That is why the Bible is available. The Bible says, "Do not be conformed to this world, but be transformed by the renewing of your minds, so that you may discern what is the will of God – what is good and acceptable and perfect." (Romans 12: 2 NRSV)

Some will say this is not fair or that there is not enough time to read the Bible. Not everyone was raised with a Sunday School teacher to understand faith. Not everybody has access to a book regarding catechism. We do not start our lives and faith in the same place. Nevertheless, wherever you are right now in your life, you must understand that the Bible is available to help you. It will even help you save time and worries! As you read the Bible, you will be making better choices and, in fact, the right choice. I encourage you to take a few minutes each day to read even just a few lines. When you read God's Word in the Bible, always ask the Holy Spirit to enlighten you while you read. Jesus gave us the Holy Spirit on Pentecost to console and guide you. He will help you. It's part of His mission. He is even your advocate; you are protected and never alone.

Some may argue that it is not necessary to take the time to understand faith and spirituality, while some believe God should do it for us. Others still may think God already did everything for us, so we don't have anything to do. It became clear to me over the years that it is our responsibility to learn and move forward both spiritually and as citizens. We must take time to read the Bible and gain control over our lives.

Most of us can easily access a Bible. After finishing my studies in Languages, I decided to take a law course. During a class, the teacher explained that, in Quebec, we could not say we are not guilty because we didn't know the law. A judge would never accept such a reason because all legal issues are televised. Since the House of Commons for federal laws and the National Assembly for the provincial laws are on television, they are easily accessible for all to experience. A television set, according to their laws, is considered an essential good. We all have the right to have access to a television. Because of this, as a citizen of Quebec, we should know the laws even though we are not lawyers.

The same concept applies to faith. We should read the Bible. It is our code of conduct *par excellence*, and it is up to us to learn it. We have a responsibility. Knowing the Word of God can protect us in all kinds of situations. The Word of God gives us the discernment we need to make good decisions in our lives. We save ourselves a lot of time and frustration by knowing the Word of God and living it. The Word of God is the foundation of our faith. Just as a good contractor knows that a solid foundation must be built first, so does a Christian need the solid foundation that the Bible provides.

God's Word points us in the right direction. It is by living in the Spirit that we find true peace. It helps us in our daily life and our spiritual journey as we learn the distinction between good and evil. All you should know about life is in the Bible. No book can surpass the Word of God. What a great treasure! We should never put it out of our sight.

I once heard a story of a young adult who wanted a car and constantly asked his father for one. For his birthday, his dad gave him a Bible. Seeing that it was not a car, the son threw the book on the ground and furiously left the house, and never returned. His dad left his son's room just as it had been left. When his dad passed away, the son came back to look after the house. When he entered his bedroom, he opened the Bible his father had given him. He picked it up from the floor where he had thrown it and found a check. His father had placed a check in the Bible to buy the car he had wanted. He was unaware of that because he had never even opened the Bible. We are often missing out on what we need because we fail to open our Bibles.

While learning about spiritual life during my stay at the Center, I came across Father Joseph-Mary Verlinde's lectures. One of his conferences dealt with his testimony that followed him from New Age teachings to the Catholic priesthood. After seeing what was false in the New Age movement through his own life experiences, he presented lectures to warn people of its dangers. After listening to Father Verlinde's testimony, his journey confirmed I was on the right track in following Jesus. I had experienced for myself that what is not from Jesus will lead you to unhappiness and death.

Back when I was trying to find New Age classes, I was tempted to try Tai Chi because the motions looked so peaceful and grace-ful. There was a group of people in my area doing Tai Chi outside, facing the sun. It looked appealing. Today, it seems that God protected me from another mistake. I would have offended God in my spiritual research by doing this. "And he brought me into the inner court of the house of the Lord; there, at the entrance of the temple of the Lord, between the porch and the altar, were about twenty-five men, with their backs to the temple of the Lord, and their faces towards the east, prostrating themselves to the sun towards the east. Then he said to me, 'Have you seen this, O mortal? It is not bad enough that the house of Judah commits the abominations done here?'" (Ezekiel 8: 16–17 NRSV) Sometimes society seems to bring out old things in a new and fresh way. They want to renew your mind and body. The best way is to read the Bible because that is the truth. Nothing else.

Tai Chi and yoga are often recommended by doctors. They are said to help with stress, mood, flexibility, energy level, etc.

However, this is not the case. The more involved you get in these activities, the more you will distance yourself from the Word of God. It will, in fact, make you emotionally unstable. Your body will feel it, and your physical state will worsen. To prevent depression and heart conditions, doctors will recommend exercise. That's sound advice, but again, do not get into the occult-like yoga to do mild exercises.

Instead of relying on an exercise like Tai Chi and yoga, what has helped me over the years is physiotherapy, the science of movement. If you have pain in any area of your body, stretching and strengthening muscles can help repair physical problems. It proved its worth to me. Physiotherapists understand the cause of the injury and have the ability to treat it without medication. It is done through movement. Health professionals provide a series of movements to stretch the injured part of the body. They will also give a different set of movements to help strengthen the muscles. By following these exercises and performing the required number of repetitions daily, relief may come quickly.

CHAPTER 5

Health

To live happier and healthier, we will have to come back to our roots. What do I mean by that? We will need to live as our ancestors did. They would eat good meat and drink fresh water. We need to try to live according to what was given to us originally. Our ancestors showed us how to work the ground and harvest. What comes from nature is healthier than what has been manipulated by people. Food that is being manufactured is not nourishing us, and, worse, it is making us unhealthy.

If you are not sure about what type of food would be good for you, ask yourself how God created it. Was it transformed? If it was transformed, look for a more natural alternative. For example, instead of buying apple juice, make your apple juice. You can also eat an apple or make a compote. By making our food just like our ancestors, we know the ingredients inside. That makes a big difference in our bodies.

Try to buy grass-fed meat. If you know local farmers in your area, you can always ask them to know if they sell their produce. Farmers should work with people's health in mind. If you see it's done like a manufacturer for profit, try to find a farmer who has your best interest in mind. When money is the goal in farming, the quality of the product is not recommended.

Natural remedies are better than medication because pills have harmful side effects. They are made by humans. There are many natural remedies available. You can do some research and pray to the Lord about it. You will see how the Spirit will guide you regarding that. "Their fruit will be for food, and their leaves for healing." (Ezekiel 47:12 NRSV) If you really need to, take medication; otherwise, the pain will be unbearable. Say a little prayer before. Thank the Lord for the medication that will give you relief, and ask Him to turn it into water that could be harmful to your health.

Always remember to love yourself the way God made you. There is no use trying to change your appearance because it will only harm you in the end. Tattoos can cause allergic reactions, skin infections, and more. Your hair color is fine the way it is. Hair dyes can irritate and cause thinning. Some people even have hair loss after using hair dyes. In the end, it's not worth it. If your goal is to have better relationships at work or in your social life, it won't work, and, in the end, you will only end up hurting yourself in the process. God created you the way you are. Learn to love yourself just as you are and accept His Love for you.

Satan does not care about our souls, nor does he care about our bodies. He wants us to die and choose him instead of Jesus. In this world, we are at war. We need to open our eyes and ears to what is around us. We are God's children. We are victorious in Jesus. God has already won, but we need to push evil back. We can resist evil by praying, fasting, attending Mass, reading the Bible, and going to Confession. In the Bible, we read, "Therefore take up the whole armour of God, so that you may be able to withstand on that evil day, and having done everything, to stand firm." (Ephesians 6:13 NRSV)

CHAPTER 6

New Age

In the New Age movement, I trusted things like crystals, energy, tetrahedron, and pendulum. These things can begin to control us and often manipulate our emotions. I remember learning about the tetrahedron from a lady I worked with. After learning all I needed to keep track of it, I was afraid to go out. Based on a calendar she gave me, there were times when it was safe for me to get out of the house, and there were times when I should not. It depended on what type of moon was on that calendar. If it was black, it was preferable not to leave the house and/or make an appointment on those days. She explained she had a car accident when the moon was black. She didn't know about the tetrahedron back then. Since she had discovered this, she considered this knowledge to be true.

Because of my ignorance, I was driven by fear, not love. From my born-again experience, I learned that fear does not come from God. So, if it doesn't come from God, who or what does it come from? It comes from Satan and demons. I had no idea it existed. I often considered Satan and the devil to be tales and legends. That is exactly what Satan wants us to believe. By thinking they do not exist, they have a lot of freedom. Yet, they must submit to our authority as children of God.

The devil does not want us to find out we are children of God. He doesn't want us to go to church. He doesn't want us to read the Bible. The demons don't want us to use the name of Jesus. Why? Because the devil wants our souls. As soon as we start practicing our Christian faith, the devil's plan just gets washed away. He can't get hold of us anymore. He's no longer capable of manipulating us. Satan does not care about us; he tries all kinds of tricks on us because he is jealous.

Jesus gave us what we need to save our souls. Jesus died for us. He shed His blood for us so we can have an abundant life. God wants us to thrive. That is why we have to fight the good fight; we must pray, we must use holy water, we must go to Mass, we must read the Bible, we must use Jesus' name, etc. The church's treasures are at our disposal. When we stand firm in the Lord, God protects us. "But David said to the Philistine, 'You come to me with sword and spear and javelin; but I come to you in the name of the Lord of hosts, the God of the armies of Israel, whom you have defied." (1 Samuel 17:45 NRSV)

Jesus is there every step of our lives. In the Catholic faith, there are seven sacraments. They are available thanks to the redeeming death of Jesus Christ. He comes into our being and lives what we live. All sacraments are blessings from God and parallel our lives: Baptism, Confession, First Communion, Confirmation, Holy Orders, Marriage, and Extreme Unction. These sacraments are provided to us so that we may maintain a connection with God.

New Age keeps us away from God and leads us to seek answers and solutions that are outside of us and not within. The true answers are all in you because God is in you. He loves His children and looks forward to our *yes*. When we live in the spirit, which means in accordance with the Word of God, we must not be afraid.

I later came across a DVD entitled '*Vatican Teaching on the New Age* by Moira Noonan. In the documentary, Mrs. Noonan explains the dangers of the New Age movement. During the conference, she talked about a document entitled "Jesus Christ the Bearer of the Water of Life" written by Pope John Paul II. He explained why the religious aspect of the New Age movement is incompatible with the Christian faith. I was happy to discover it, but I was saddened in a way because I never knew this document existed.

Having studied both New Age and the Catholic faith, I could compare these two beliefs. What did I get out of the New Age movement? Depression, confusion, shame, and unhappiness. What has Christianity given me? It has given me life and healed my shame. I am happy. I have well-intentioned friends. I feel like a member of a group, and now I have found my best friend, Jesus, the True Bearer of Life!

I remember attending a New Age conference, and one lady was saying she was in communication with Merlin the Magician. It felt wrong, but I couldn't explain why at the time. In Christianity, we learn that magic is deception. This lady was not free. She was following a spirit that was not holy. We have to focus on Jesus and His Word to be free. "Do not turn to mediums or wizards, do not seek them out, to be defiled by them: I am Yahweh your God." (Leviticus 19:31 NRSV)

The New Age movement makes us live our lives contrary to the way we are created. The movement encourages people to concentrate on themselves, their breathing, their well-being, etc. However, our world is built on love, God's Love. To live happily, love must flow freely among us. When we have compassion towards others, we feel we are helping the world in a positive way. This brings us true happiness because we are made to love. When we follow the teachings of our Master, our God, God opens our hearts. "Love is patient; love is kind; love is not envious or boastful or arrogant or rude. It does not insist on its own way; it is not irritable or resentful; it does not rejoice in wrongdoing, but rejoices in the truth. It bears all things, believes all things, hopes all things, endures all things. Love never ends [. . .]. (1 Corinthians 13:4–8 NRSV)

Even if these practices are done with the best of intentions, all these people are letting the devil in their lives, not God. How? Because they are not doing the will of God. They are leading others astray. People in the New Age movement want to help us, but it is not according to the Word of God. We are God's children; the Lord has given us the Church and the Bible. We have to learn God's teachings because they are aimed at protecting us and never restricting us. The only spirit we need to follow is the Holy Spirit.

When we believe and trust in God, Jesus inspires us. This inspiration could come from dreams but not from exterior signs. The answers will come from within you. St. Joseph was warned of what was to come for both he and Mary in various dreams. We clearly can read these passages in Matt.1:18, Matt. 2:13, Matt. 2:19, and Matt. 2:22. St. Joseph carried out God's will without hesitation. Just like St. Joseph, Jesus wants to help you at this present moment. He will guide you and help you speak to the people you need to talk to. He will give you what you need to move forward positively. You are a child of God.

Both the Old and New Testaments are excellent to read. I later also discovered books regarding Bible concordances. The biblical words are set up in alphabetical order, just like a dictionary. By looking up a word, the concordance will refer to all the Bible verses pertaining to the word you are looking for. Let's say you would like to know more about "hope." When you look up that word; it will give you a complete list of Bible verses related to "hope." The references written in red are the passages spoken by Jesus Himself. Of course, we can't assume something from just a few passages. We must truly understand the Bible. The best way to have a good understanding of the individual Bible verses or passages is to read the Bible.

I decided to take another holiday. Checking the calendar, I randomly decided to take one week in August. I had no destination, but I was hoping to find a place. When I read the newspaper, I noticed an ad from a travel agency. They were inviting people to a conference to learn about various tourist trips they had planned for the year. I signed up right away to attend the meeting. At the end of the presentation, I realized there were no guided tours during the week I had chosen. What's more, there was no trip of interest to me. I wanted to visit a shrine and pray to the Virgin Mary. Because I couldn't afford to go abroad, I needed to find a place in Canada.

One Saturday morning at the restaurant, Mark was sharing a few photos. Assuming they were family pictures, they didn't interest me right away. I just kept on eating and talking. When I finally looked at the pictures, I realized they were pictures of a pilgrimage. That changed everything! I started asking Mark about it. He explained that the Virgin Mary appeared to Father Melvin Doucette, asking him to build a small chapel to pray and feel God's Love. This was precisely what I was looking for! Since Mark just came back from that trip, I was expecting him to go back next year. Seeing my interest, he said the next trip would be in August. I inquired about the exact days. It was the same week I had picked for my holiday. Mother Mary placed this pilgrimage in my heart! I was amazed! As I sometimes call it, "That's certainly a wink from Heaven!"

I asked Mark if I could be a part of the next group. He told me he was having a problem with this trip because he was missing a driver for one of the leased vehicles. Due to the number of pilgrims, he needed to rent two vans. That was the easiest problem to solve. I volunteered to become the other driver. He agreed right away. We were on our way to Prince Edward Island! Thank you, Mother Mary!

When we arrived at P.E.I., we went into the prayer room. In the little chapel, Father Melvin Doucette gave his testimony. Father Melvin grew up in Prince Edward Island and became a missionary in Africa. He worked as a priest for several years. Because of his mother's precarious health, he returned to P.E.I. to take care of her. During that time, the Virgin Mary appeared to Fr. Doucette. She asked him to build the chapel we were in to greet pilgrims, so they could pray. Obediently, he said he wanted to do it. However, he explained that he didn't have the money to complete such a project. He said he was as "poor as a church rat." She said she was going to take care of the details, and she did.

The architectural plan for the chapel was revealed to a Montrealer. After receiving the revelation, he drew it on paper. He even knew who to hand it to. He went to P.E.I. as soon as he could with his tools and the diagram in the trunk of his car. When he found Fr. Doucette, he explained that he wasn't ready because he didn't have the resources to build yet. The Montrealer gave the plans to Fr. Doucette. He asked to be notified as soon as he was ready to build. Fr. Melvin agreed to maintain contact. During that time, he was able to meet a few contractors to determine how much it would cost to build the prayer room.

Later, a man from the United States felt the need to go to P.E.I. to give a large amount of money to Father Doucette. He did not know why, but he was led to give a big sum of money by check. To Father Melvin's surprise, the amount covered exactly what he needed to build the chapel. He contacted the Montrealer and the contractor to start building. Many volunteers came to help complete this project.

The painting of Our Lady of Prince Edward Island found in the prayer room also happened miraculously. An artist nearby felt that she should paint an image of the Virgin Mary. She began to paint and, to her astonishment, felt that each brushstroke was guided. When she completed the painting, she had to wait for the right person to claim it. She had no idea who it was for. One day, Father Melvin felt like stopping at a specific house. He went to the door and knocked. The woman opened the door, and he explained that he was looking for a painting. Ah! She said, "I've been waiting for you for a long time now." They didn't even know each other. The Blessed Mother Mary indeed took care of all details. She was given the name of Our Lady of Prince Edward Island. When we look at the painting, we can see she is standing on the Island. It was amazing to hear and see all of the miracles still taking place.

In the second part of our pilgrimage, Father Melvin gave a lecture regarding the importance of following God's Ten Commandments. He explained that these rules could be compared to traffic codes. To prevent accidents at the wheel, it is necessary to know and follow them on the road. The same goes for life. If we respect the Ten Commandments of God, God can protect us from all evil here on Earth. He showed us the book *Catechism of the Catholic Church*. This book explains in detail the Ten Commandments and the Creed. The Creed is a prayer that contains 12 truths. It came from the 12 apostles.

As Father Doucette was explaining the teaching of the Catholic faith, I started to cry. I was sitting in the back of the prayer room, and my tears wouldn't stop falling. At one point, he talked about the gift of tears. I didn't think this was concerning me, but I was certainly crying. Hearing the truth from a priest brought me great consolation. It certainly helped me to stay in my faith and continue trusting in God.

Father Melvin also revealed to us that day that Mother Mary requested a monastery for men and women be built there. Though it is not built yet, the land necessary to build was generously donated by his neighbor. While we were there, he showed us the religious habit of the religious order and explained that Mother Mary even blessed a water source on this site.

When I came back home from this wonderful pilgrimage, I felt so blessed. With all the teachings I had, I kept moving forward with the beliefs of the church. Mark kept showing me the wonders of the Catholic faith and took me to different prayer gatherings. I discovered a local chapel of worship and found a religious community that would invite all the attendees to hear a preacher once a month. We could eat together, talk, and go to confession. It was like going on vacation each time.

During that time, I discovered a beautiful Bible story about our Father's Love and mercy towards all of us. "[. . .] There was a man who had two sons. The younger of them said to his father, "Father, give me the share of the property that will belong to me.'

So he divided his property between them. A few days later the younger son gathered all he had and travelled to a distant country, and there he squandered his property in dissolute living. When he had spent everything, a severe famine took place throughout that country, and he began to be in need. So he went and hired himself out to one of the citizens of that country, who sent him to his fields to feed the pigs. He would gladly have filled himself with the pods that the pigs were eating, and no one gave him anything. But when he came to himself, he said, 'How many of my father's hired hands have bread enough and to spare, but here I am dying of hunger! I will get up and go to my father, and I will say to him, 'Father, I have sinned against heaven and before you, I am no longer worthy to be called your son; treat me like one of your hired hands.'' So he set off and went to his father. But while he was still far off, his father saw him and was filled with compassion; he ran and put his arms around him and kissed him. Then the son said to him, 'Father, I have sinned against heaven and before you; I am no longer worthy to be called your son.' But the father said to his slaves, 'Quickly, bring out a robe-the best one – and put it on him; put a ring on his finger and sandals on his feet. And get the fatted calf and kill it, and let us eat and celebrate; for this son of mine was dead and is alive again; he was lost and is found!' And they began to celebrate" (Luke 15: 11–32 NRSV). How much like God was this earthly father in his love for his child!

After experiencing all this change in my life, I began to sense a certain withdrawal from office work. I didn't understand why because things were going so well. I enjoyed all the team members I worked with. I was able to share my spiritual discoveries with them, and they responded positively. This was useful for both them and me. My faith grew stronger. We have such a marvelous God! When we start following God, our faith gets tested. We have to stay firm in our faith and believe in God's Word.

God always works for the greater good of all His children. My tasks at work became difficult to carry out, and my motivation was low. My fatigue increased so much that it became unbearable. In my heart, I could feel the Lord asking me to leave my job. I thought, "This is not possible! How can God ask me to do this?" I could not say *yes* so easily now. I didn't want to quit.

Up until this point, my work had been going well; each task was so well-organized. It was a pleasure working there. Yet as time passed, each task became a burden. A few weeks later, I told the Lord that if He wanted me to resign, He needed to tell me. I had to hear it from Him; if not, I could not give my *yes*. Since I had seen a documentary about Sister Faustina's life, I knew that Jesus could talk to us. Thinking this was not going to happen to me, I continued working at my job without worrying about leaving, though I still felt quite tired and demotivated.

A couple of weeks later, I had to go to the production area to distribute reports. This area was filled with industrial machines, which were all working at full capacity. After posting the reports, I started leaving that place quickly, thinking of my next tasks. Suddenly, I heard these words, "Stop making me suffer; resign to serve God!" Was it possible? The voice was so clear, despite all the machinery surrounding me. I couldn't believe it! Was this my imagination or a plan from Satan? Did the Lord truly speak to me at such an unexpected time? The noise from the machinery was so loud that it was hard to concentrate and even harder to hear a team member talk. Yet, the voice I heard was clear and easy to understand. The voice came from within.

God wanted me in another place. Despite this great sign full of love, it was still hard to say *yes*. It made me sad, but at the same time, I knew it was the perfect will of God. It was with great trust in the Lord that I gave my resignation to my supervisor. What was ahead of me was unknown. I gave myself entirely to God. I kept on thinking of this Bible verse that was the stronghold that helped me move forward in faith:

"Then he said to them all, 'If any want to become my followers, let them deny themselves and take up their cross daily and follow me'" (Luke 9:23 NRSV). I chose to follow Him.

Now I had to discern God's will from here. I had no idea what to expect, which was so difficult. Did God want me to be religious? I didn't know exactly. I was thankful that Mark took my decision seriously. He wanted to help me find the will of God. I found this reassuring. I told him one day that he was like an angel on my path. It would be strange for him to hear me say that. He said that, typically, people say he's like a father. In my opinion, though, he was definitely an angel.

One time, Mark invited me to go to Greensides Farm in Marmora, Ontario. There was an organized bus going there on December 8, which is the Feast of the Immaculate Conception. This is a day Catholics celebrate to acknowledge that Mother Mary conceived without sin. In 1854, Pope Pius IX explained the importance of the Immaculate Conception. Since I was available that day and needed answers to my prayers, I wanted to bring all my intentions to the Blessed Virgin Mary by asking her for help and advice since I had once heard that Jesus could not refuse anything that came from His Mother.

On the day of the pilgrimage, I attended Mass at the Basilica Cathedral of St. Cecilia in Valleyfield, Quebec, Canada. It took place in the crypt early in the morning. As soon as we stepped out of the church, I noticed the bus was already waiting. From there, we went to St. Joseph's Oratory in Montreal to pick up more passengers. On the road, we prayed the Rosary.

During prayer, I started to feel very tired. I fell asleep on the bus. This was unusual since it was the beginning of the day. Suddenly, the bus started to hit potholes. As I was waking up, I heard angels singing and smelled roses. What a beautiful awakening! I was so amazed to smell such a scent when hearing angels sing. It was surely like Heaven. The smell of the flowers was so strong that the bus driver lowered his window to freshen the air. The odor of roses stayed until we arrived at Greensides Farm.

Mark, who was the animator during the trip, asked if others smelled the roses. I was happy to hear him ask the other passengers. I didn't know what was going on. I had kept this experience to myself. To my surprise, others smelled the same thing as me. What was special was that the first two or three rows of people, including the driver, smelt it. And the last two or three rows of people in the back of the bus also smelt it. What a beautiful spiritual experience! I will always cherish that moment in my heart.

Since I lost track of time and direction because I had fallen asleep, I realized that we had arrived. I was enjoying the experience so much that I did not want to leave the bus. However, when the bus stopped, and the pilgrims got out of their seats, I felt like I had to do the same thing. Even though I wanted to stay and enjoy this heavenly experience, I followed the others and stepped off the bus. I didn't know what to expect as I had never been there before. I didn't even look on the Internet beforehand to see what it looked like.

I found out that the owner wanted pilgrims to pray to Mother Mary, just like in Medjugorje. So, there is a Rosary path and a Way of the Cross. The Way of the Cross helps us not to take Jesus' sacrifice for granted. It brings us back to Jesus' time when He was condemned and died on the cross for all our sins. These meditations help us to follow in Christ's footsteps. It also helps us realize that we must accept our sufferings and give them to God as soon as we feel the weight of the burden.

The Station of the Cross helps us to meditate on the agony of Jesus. He bore all our sins and made us free. This means that we are free from Satan. We're not the victims, as we have Jesus' name now. This is an enormous blessing! Thank you, Jesus, for your Love and Divine Mercy! Some may think that because Jesus sacrificed it all for us, we have nothing left to do. They believe you simply have to live your life without thinking about it. This is not what life is all about. Because Christ died on our behalf, we belong to Him. He wants us to walk with Him by being united with Him. We can develop an intimate relationship by praying, worshipping, going to church, confessing our sins, reading the Bible, singing, talking to Him, obeying Him, etc. By being in a state of grace, God can protect us. Jesus is a person, and He is a friend. He is your BEST Friend. He is your Creator. He knows you more than anyone else. You must follow Him and trust Him. This is how we live in peace and have real happiness. The devil is still in the world. We need God to protect us all the time. We are created by Him and for Him.

After returning from Marmora, Mark mentioned a religious community for young adults in Sherbrooke, Quebec. He drove me there, and I had the opportunity to talk to the founder. After explaining my conversion and taking some time to think, he agreed to let me live with them for an undetermined period. I was happy because I needed time to discern God's mission for me. Seeking the will of God requires long moments of intimacy with Him.

The first time I ate with the community, a girl who had been sitting beside me suddenly decided to move and sat right in front of me. To start the conversation, she wanted to know what led me to the community. I was embarrassed to tell my story. I explained to her that I had resigned from my job to answer a call from the Lord. I was nervous to hear her reaction. She answered, "That's precisely what I'm going through!" I was so relieved! It's as though the Lord removed all my doubts and fears to continue in faith. I felt like an enormous weight was being lifted off my shoulders. The conversation was so helpful! At the end of our discussion, I thanked her for bringing me such relief. She answered that she was praying to the Holy Spirit. That explained everything! I could see God's amazing power in this. Rather than being ridiculed and misunderstood, I felt I was in the right place. Thank you, Lord!

A month before Christmas, the Community had to finalize an event. Each year, music and sketches were prepared, and they would open their doors to the public. I was able to help in the kitchen by doing the dishes, cutting vegetables, etc. I was happy, but at the same time, I felt unsure about the future. I would sometimes say I felt like I was in a void. At the same time, I was surrounded by God's Love. My future was not empty; it was full of Love. This would always bring me comfort. I was in God's hands, and that was enough to put my mind at ease. The dedication of those young adults showed me their love for Jesus. This helped me see our mission: to make God known and loved, whether by singing, talking, or helping in our daily lives.

One week before Christmas, I left the community and went to my parents' home. It was great to be back with my family and friends. Living Christmas with faith around people I loved made me enjoy Jesus' many blessings. On December 25th, Christians celebrate the birth of Jesus, our Saviour, who was born to take the human condition to show us how to be happy in this life and the next.

A new year was starting. It was entirely in the hands of the Lord. I didn't know where to go or what to do, but I trusted Him. I told myself that by praying and going to church, the Lord would show me the way. I made sure I attended Mass on the first Friday of each month. This Mass is in honor of the Sacred Heart. There are so many beautiful promises regarding this Mass that had been revealed to St. Marguerite-Mary Alacoque, a Catholic nun and a mystic, from the Visitation Convent in Paray-le-Monial in France.

One day, I went to the chapel at St. Anne's Hospital in Sainte-Anne-de-Bellevue, QC. The parish priest who took care of the Sainte-Anne church also took care of the hospital. It is a hospital for veterans, but everyone was welcome to attend Mass there. When I showed up, I noticed that Mark was already praying. I sat beside him. During Mass, I started to get dizzy. I had the impression of losing my balance. It's as if the tiles beneath my feet were lifting. I didn't know what was happening. When Mass ended, Mark and I went to the parking lot without talking. I could see he was upset about something, but I didn't know what it was. He wanted to say something, but it seemed the words failed him.

On my way home, I felt a need to distance myself from Mark. That didn't make any sense to me. The only one who could keep me from praying was the devil. "This is all wrong," I said to myself. How can I avoid a friend who helped me discover so many beautiful treasures of the Church, including Mass, spiritual retreats, rosary, pilgrimages, novenas, chapels of worship, evenings of prayer, praying in tongues, the Bible, sanctuaries, Saints, and Religious Communities? I did not understand, yet the idea of staying far from him was very persistent.

The dizziness became stronger. It was even hard for me to breathe. I felt so uncomfortable that I had to lie down. A few hours later, the phone rang, and it was Mark. He called me to know if I would like to attend a prayer meeting. Ever since I met Mark, I had never refused to pray with him, but this time my health and negative thoughts made me say no, even though it was incredibly difficult. It made no sense. He understood and said, "We're going to postpone this for another time." I agreed and hung up the telephone, confused.

The next day, his wife called me to say that Mark had passed away during the night. I was so touched by the news that I cried for three days. I had finally met a friend with good intentions, and now he was gone with Jesus. I was so sad! I could only do one thing from this moment forward: follow Jesus alone. He is my greatest friend. During the wake, I was pleasantly surprised to hear that two of his children, who were far from Jesus, became believers. They had a born-again experience. It showed me that Mark was still active spiritually on the other side. Even if I couldn't see him anymore, I knew I could still depend on my angel sent from God.

A few months after, I decided to attend a spiritual retreat in Plantagenet, Ontario, Canada. The name of the center is "Centre de l'Amour." During my stay, the founder announced that she needed volunteers to enlarge the cafeteria. At the end of the retreat, I made an appointment with her. I wanted to participate in the project. In the meantime, I felt this would be an excellent opportunity to pray to know the perfect will of God in my life. I volunteered my skills to help in the kitchen, laundry, and office. While I was talking with her, I sensed she was uncomfortable with the idea. I still gave her my telephone number, but I didn't expect anything from it.

A few days later, the founder called me. To my surprise, she needed my help. The following day, I left to go to the Center for an undetermined period. My duties consisted of helping in the office, helping cook, and washing the dishes. During my first meal with the staff and volunteers, a large group of pilgrims came in. This was unexpected according to the founder's calendar. They were supposed to show up one day later. Teenagers just kept on coming into the kitchen, and they were hungry! We had to move fast to serve all of them. It was busy throughout the weekend. Since we were already behind schedule, we were struggling to make ends meet. I ended up in the back of the kitchen scrubbing large pots and pans. Behind me was an unknown volunteer who was also washing dishes. While I was rubbing the pots and pans, I realized I didn't have rubber gloves, and I was trying to find some to protect my hands.

As I looked around and under the sink, this gentleman approached me and said, "You don't have . . ." Not giving him a chance to finish his sentence, I told him, "Yes, I don't have any rubber gloves." He answered, "No, you don't have a wedding ring." That was completely unexpected! I was astonished! Who was this man? Besides not wearing gloves, I also didn't have a wedding ring! What could this all mean?

CHAPTER 7

The Relationship

At this point, gloves weren't my focus anymore. My attention shifted entirely. As I was talking to him, I learned that his name was George. While doing the dishes, he asked me a few questions about my life. Poor him, I told myself. He may not understand what I'm saying. I was in the back of a kitchen with neither a job nor direction. I explained to him that I wanted to be a witness of Jesus as a consecrated layperson. I didn't know how he would react to that, but it was my situation.

I asked him some questions as well. I found out that he came from Sherbrooke, Quebec, to help the Center voluntarily, just like me. But, in his case, he drove about four hours to be where we were. He would take care of the landscaping and the machinery. I saw in front of me a man with a great big heart, and I felt he understood me.

George invited me to a restaurant the next day for dinner after we finished the dishes. I was pleased to accept the offer. The following morning, the weather was already hot. This was unusual in Ontario, Canada, even during summer. I went to the chapel to attend Mass. I noticed that George had already arrived. Because it was so hot that day, the elderly priest was not able to show up. So, I wished George a good day, telling him that I was looking forward to seeing him that evening. From the moment he went out to work, a million uncertainties crossed my mind. I gave what I was feeling to God, and I tried to concentrate on my job first.

The day was busy. There were many pilgrims at the Center, and there was a lot to do. Each task had to be done quickly. Suddenly, I realized that 10 a.m. had already passed. It was time for me to look after the snacks. I snuck into the conference room silently. I didn't want to interrupt anything. The speaker was talking to teens. He explained that, even if they wanted to go on a mission, they had to remain open to meeting people. Even if they had a call to serve the Lord, that didn't necessarily mean that they would become a priest or a nun. Marriage or remaining single was also a vocation. It's just like a consecrated life. These vocations are quite different but equally important.

I left that room somewhat perplexed. I felt that those words were not only applicable to those teenagers. This explanation applied to me as well. That was strange. It seemed that the Lord allowed me to hear these words to persuade me to give George a chance. I was under the impression that Jesus was saying, "Do not be afraid. Trust Me. I am guiding you."

Later in the day, the founder announced to the staff and volunteers that Mass would be held after dinner. From where I was, I could see George through a window. He was working hard mowing the grass on a hot summer day. At the end of the day, we both got ready for our evening. We finished all the dishes, and it was now time for our date. What joy! What was awaiting us? I didn't know, but I sensed Jesus was there.

As we were about to leave, I asked him if he wanted to attend Mass before our dinner. I knew I was asking almost the impossible. We were both hungry and tired. I told myself that if we put the Lord first from our first date, God would never abandon us. After a moment of reflection, he agreed, even though he already had the car started with the air conditioner running.

After Mass, we went to a small restaurant in town to talk. While we were talking, we realized we both lived similar stories. I told him about my conversion. To my amazement, it did not surprise him. I realized George was open to spirituality, and this put me at ease. He knew God could do anything; He could even change hearts. After talking some more, he explained that he was working as an employee for a religious community in Sherbrooke.

At the end of our discussion, we set another date for the following week. He went back to Sherbrooke, and I kept helping out at the Spiritual Center. Each weekend we spent together was always so enjoyable. It felt like Heaven; our rendezvous was perfect. He often spoke about his experiences in the military, serving for approximately ten years as a cook. During those years, he traveled extensively and was confronted with various interesting situations. His stories would always grab my attention.

Over time, we felt like we were made for each other. We felt that God made it possible for us to know one another. This made our love even purer and more wonderful.

A few weeks later, a woman considered as a "privileged of St. Anne" came to talk about the Blessed Virgin Mary's mother. Since we were already on site, we were able to listen to the whole conference. We stopped volunteering during the weekend to listen to the teachings. We felt we had to listen to the teachings. At the end of the retreat, we felt stronger as a couple. We knew we could build our lives by anchoring ourselves to Jesus Christ. Even though this wouldn't prevent the difficulties ahead, we felt we were equipped for our future together. Because Jesus brought us together, we thought we would always put Him first. We knew that what was outside of Jesus was dark and lifeless.

George really enjoyed nature. He made me discover so many beautiful aspects of life. For instance, he liked to pick blueberries in the wild. He had found a place in the middle of the Quebec province where nature surrounded us. We were far from civilization. All our worries went away when we were there. It felt like a big weight off our shoulders. We didn't feel any pressure from anybody. We could simply be ourselves. We felt free. It was such a relief that it would make us cry.

At the blueberry patch, there were so many blueberry bushes! It was nice to see all the blueberries on these little bushes. George told me that they reminded him of Mother Mary. The blueberries would grow like a pyramid and were light blue in the wild. They really did look like little statues of Mother Mary. He would sometimes feel bad taking the blueberries from the branches. But it was for a good cause. He would give them to a religious community nearby. The nuns from the community explained to him one day that the blueberries healed one of the sisters from a disease.

While he was picking the fruits, he used to hold his rosary in one hand and pick the blueberries in the other. I always wondered how he managed to do that with just one hand! He used to tell me the adventures he had had while picking them. He came face-to-face with a bear once. He also saw a skunk walk right between his legs. His stories were so funny!

At night, we could see the stars! How beautiful that was! The sky was so clear, and the stars were so bright! He liked to discover God's creation. This is one of the reasons why he wanted to work in the army. He wanted to discover the world. He traveled to the point of contentment. I was simply happy to hear all about his adventures, and we would take pleasure in talking about it.

The more time went by, the more we felt God wanted us to continue our lives together. We decided to make an appointment with the priest taking care of the Sainte-Anne-de-Bellevue Church. George and I wanted to get married at the end of September. The priest looked at his agenda, but he wasn't available. He said that he had an opening on the first Saturday of October. The priest said it would fall on the feast day of Our Lady of the Rosary. George and I looked at one another, thinking that would be perfect. As we were talking to our friends about the wedding and the house we were about to buy, they asked us what the name of our new parish was. Since we were still going to Saint Anne and the paperwork was underway, we didn't know exactly. One day, we decided to find the nearest church in our area. George and I could hardly believe it. It was called Lady of the Rosary.

Once more, this confirmed that our marriage was certainly willed by God. Our dear St. Anne was certainly making sure things were in place for George and me to grow together. Since we had to set up the readings for the ceremony, I talked to the priest about wanting it to resemble that of Medjugorje. The weddings there focus on one thing: Jesus' Cross. This means there was a cross between George and me during the wedding. Before embracing one another, we kissed the cross first. Our marriage wasn't just two people, but it consisted of three now. Jesus was now with us in our marriage.

After the wedding, George and I walked together in faith, putting Christ first. We had a little prayer area where we would say our daily rosary together in front of a cross. We attended Mass each Sunday to thank God for our week and to give Him the week that awaited us. I found a full-time job in Sainte-Anne-de-Bellevue. Like all couples, we had our ups and downs.

Not even a week after our wedding, George fell into a depression. He had to be hospitalized. We didn't have a honeymoon. I remember a coworker laughing at me, thinking this was very strange. I continued trusting in God. I wanted to accept the cross God had given me. I wanted to help George the best way I knew how, and that was to love George in Jesus Christ. God carried His cross to the end, and that was my intention as well. I wanted to respect my wedding vow of in sickness and in health. I would remain faithful to my husband.

We felt greatly strengthened through prayer. Real happiness was having God in our lives. Some of the difficulties we encountered seemed insurmountable, but with prayer, it became easier. I knew I wasn't alone.

At times, during or after our prayers, we would be enlightened to do something we wouldn't have thought about. Without divine help, nobody can succeed or even move forward in life. St. Teresa of Lisieux once said, "Everything is a blessing." Since my conversion, I have always focused on that statement. If God allows us to experience joy or sadness, we must be certain that it is there to help us walk in faith, in love, and with the knowledge of God. Our sufferings help us enter into the mystery of love, for they become blessings. It is important to welcome our experiences and give them to the Father in union with Jesus. Our suffering helps us go to the source of Love.

After two years of marriage, we felt ready to have children. Month after month, I was surprised to find that I wasn't pregnant. The results remained negative. I was deeply saddened by that, but I learned a lot during that time. I've realized that no birth is a coincidence. Life comes from the Lord and is not a mistake. All of us are valuable in the eyes of God. Life needs to be treasured.

When we realized we could not have children at that time, we decided to welcome foreign students into our home. The purpose of this program was to help students learn French. We worked hard to complete the renovations of our house to welcome them. Two weeks after their arrival, they asked to be transferred to another foster family in Quebec. They preferred living in Montreal. Despite this disappointment, we thanked Jesus for what was happening to us. George and I were sad. We worked hard to make sure the students would be happy. Immediately after they left, we went into our prayer room and said the Lord's prayer with a heavy heart in front of the cross.

A few months before the students' arrival, George and I read the book *Power in Praise* by Merlin R. Carothers. The author teaches us that no matter what our difficulties are, there are also a lot of blessings. We must trust in the Lord's Word. Our stronghold comes from the Bible: "Rejoice always, pray without ceasing, give thanks in all circumstances; for this is the will of God in Christ Jesus for you" (1 Thessalonians 5:16–18 NRSV).

After that, I started reading another book describing the Gospel. The revelations came from Maria Valtorta. The title of the book was *The Gospel as Revealed to Me* (The original title was *The Poem of the Man-God*.) The beginning of Volume 1 talks about St. Anne and her sadness over not having any children. The pain she was experiencing was so much like my own. I wept when I read those lines. To my astonishment, two weeks later, my body gave me different sensations. I began to feel like I might be pregnant. It was too soon to confirm, but I sensed it in my heart.

Days and weeks went by. George and I reached another peak of happiness. I was now pregnant! It felt like a miracle!

After two years of prayer, our wish became a reality. In only a few weeks, God changed our sorrow into a lot of joy. Thank you, good St. Anne, for your intercession! To my surprise, when I had my first appointment with the gynecologist, the doctor started talking about abortion. George and I had a big age difference. He was in his fifties, and I was in my thirties. The doctor was cautioning me about health issues. I wasn't worried. I said to her that the baby was a gift from God. Each child brings love and joy. My mind was made up. Regardless of the doctor's recommendations, I wanted to keep the child. Even though she continued giving her speech the way she had memorized it from beginning to end, it didn't change our conviction. Both George and I wanted this child. Life comes from God; we both knew that.

A little more than nine months later, the Lord gave us a healthy baby boy to love and nurture. George and I were very happy. We both wanted to share our faith with our child. This became our priority. We wanted to take our role as parents very seriously.

CHAPTER 8

The School

During my pregnancy, I read the encyclical *Familiaris Consortio* written by Pope John Paul II. The subtitle is *The Role of the Christian Family in the Modern World.* In this book, I learned how to love my family. It is by sharing my faith with them that they learn to love Jesus. Education was still very important to me. Since I had just discovered that Christian schools exist, we wanted to make it our priority to send our child to one. It never occurred to me before just how important a child's education and instruction are. This book opened my eyes. The pope even mentioned universities. How exciting and beautiful! This was simply the best environment to perfect our knowledge. After reading this encyclical, we simply had to find a school that was teaching what we believed.

During my pregnancy, we began looking for a Catholic school nearby. There was one at Rigaud, but after a brief discussion, I realized that they taught many other beliefs as well. We felt this would simply confuse our child. At the time, Quebec education did not consider what was so important in the past, which was faith. Our ancestors took such pride in talking about Jesus. For at least six years, we searched for an affordable Christian school near us, but nothing came out of it.

When the time came, we decided to enroll our son in the nearest public school. We had many doubts, but we were willing to try. However, from the moment school began, we immediately felt that this was not his place. The teachings and the readings failed to represent our beliefs. It was a sad turn of events for us.

Over the years, public education in Quebec became secularized. Rather than moving according to God's teachings, they taught students not to live according to God's will. In 1960, Quebec had to face great changes. During those years, the Quiet Revolution took place. This revolution changed the healthcare and education system. The government didn't want the church to take care of these two areas anymore. These fields became secularized, thus removing the nuns and priests. They even removed the crosses in the schools, and the teachers could not speak about Jesus. Similarly, in July 2019, the crucifix in the Quebec National Assembly was also removed.

Continuing our research, we found a few privately owned Christian schools. They were far away and very expensive. Regardless of that, we were prepared to move for our son's happiness. Though we were visiting areas looking for a new house, none of the places we visited seemed right. It was a difficult time because George fell into another depression. The pressure of raising our child was too much for him. He wished things could be different. I kept reminding him to trust in the Lord. There was no problem without a solution from God.

At the time, my parents were looking after my grandmother, who lived in Ontario. She was diagnosed with Alzheimer's disease. Because she was at the final stage, she had to stay in a long-term retirement home. My parents were overwhelmed with work. They had to worry about my grandmother and her house. After talking to them about the school, my mother spoke to me about my grandmother's house. She said that since the house was empty, it might be an opportunity for us to see how the schools in the region would be. This was a good idea since the Ontario education system still offers a choice to the parents. We had the option of sending our children either to a Catholic or a secular school.

We applied to the nearest Catholic school. We were hoping and praying that this would be a positive change. As the year progressed, though, we were disappointed. There was a lot of friction right from the beginning. Our son was only in the second grade. The competition was strong, and the intimidation was unthinkable. Moreover, Catholic teachings were scarcely taught.

Instead of making learning fun and welcoming, the system made it unpleasant. Instead of teaching children to be peaceful, they encouraged them to participate in karate classes. Instead of having them read spiritual texts, they had them read about magic and fairy tales. Instead of putting God and their neighbor first, they would make them compete. Instead of offering them a balanced spiritual life centered on the Bible, they had them practice yoga centering on themselves. At the end of the year, an email was sent to all the parents regarding family violence. It was concerning the children hurting the parents. Is there any wonder after a year like this?

It is important to take care of all aspects of your life. For instance, I need to look after my health. God gave me a body to take care of. To be healthy, I must exercise and make healthy meals. It won't happen on its own. The same can be said about our spiritual life. We need to take care of it by starting with God's Word. It is our spiritual nourishment.

These schools have a big responsibility, but they are not alone. They have Jesus to make it successful. With Jesus, who can fail? The authorities are drifting away from their priorities. In the end, the children are suffering, and the learning environment isn't positive. Being in charge of children is a huge task. Jesus needs to be at the head of the education system. We should give life to children, not the death of their souls! How can the next generation be happy with such teachings? How can we reduce suicide rates? How can we eliminate addictions? Simple, with Jesus' help. We cannot move forward until we understand that and accept it. That's where the power is. The power of Love! That is God's Kingdom. We need to put Jesus' word first, especially in school and especially if the school is Catholic.

One day, our son came home from school saying his backpack had been stolen. George brought him back to school immediately.

He spoke to the principal about the situation. They found it in another child's locker. The principal said he would do something about the situation, but he never did. It was the end of the year, and the principal was being transferred to another school. I phoned the police for information on bullying, and, to be honest; our discussion didn't lead anywhere. It seemed that our son had to fight for what was taken from him. He was only seven years old at the time. How are we to grow in love and peace with this kind of environment? I had had enough. From that point forward, I decided to teach my son at home. I had no idea who to contact at first, but I was determined to do it myself since it's the parent's responsibility to teach faith to our children. I had completed a bachelor's and a certificate in Languages, so I felt confident I was up to this task. I was happy to have the opportunity to share what I had learned over the years with my son.

Previously, my son had never been sent to daycare. I knew from reading spiritual books that children need to feel their parent's love as they grow up. It is when they are babies that they need to feel that security the most. They don't need another computer game, toy, or trip. They need to know their parents are there for them. How can the child know love if we do not give it to them when they are young? We made a lot of sacrifices to make sure one of his parents was there to raise him and not let strangers with their differing points of view take care of our child. We wanted him to know what true love meant.

I sent a letter to the school board requesting permission to homeschool. A little later, I was given a positive response. I started preparing all his courses. It was hard at first, but I was gaining experience. During my research, I found online Christian schools, textbooks, and the curriculum. They are all available on the Internet. Using all these resources, I could move forward with homeschooling our son.

When COVID-19 began, we did not feel the impact of those waves when schools closed. Homeschooling proved to be an excellent idea and a blessing. We did our best each day. We kept motivated by focusing on the Will of God. We could attend Mass each morning by listening to it online. Praying first thing in the morning is the best thing we can do. We recognize that God is the source of our lives. Without God's Love, I wouldn't have been able to teach my son at home. Everything comes from Him. It doesn't come from us. Without the Lord, we are nothing. We need Him all the time because we were created by Him.

"In those days Hezekiah became sick and was at the point of death. The prophet Isaiah son of Amoz came to him, and said to him, 'Thus says the Lord: Set your house in order, for you shall die; you shall not recover.' Then Hezekiah turned his face to the wall, and prayed to the Lord: 'Remember now, O Lord, I implore you, how I have walked before you in faithfulness with a whole heart, and have done what is good in your sight.' And Hezekiah wept bitterly. Then the word of the Lord came to Isaiah: 'Go and say to Hezekiah, Thus says the Lord, the God of your ancestor David: I have heard your prayer, I have seen your tears; I will add fifteen years to your life. I will deliver you and this city out of the hand of the king of Assyria, and defend this city'" (Isaiah 38: 1–6 NRSV).

As was true with Hezekiah, if God wants us to do something to serve His children, He will do it. He has the power to give life! He can do everything He wishes if it's according to our Father's plan. He can call us to do something even if we have never even studied the field. He will give us the tools, the material, the resources, and the manpower to accomplish His Will. It will not fall from the sky. We have to work hard, but He will give us the blessings we need to do it one day at a time. We depend on God, not on ourselves. We were bought back at a great price. We belong to God; we are His children.

Before George and I got married, George heard a story about a brother who had built a church in northern Canada. The builder felt inspired to build this church like an igloo. He finished the building, and it was as he had imagined. After the construction was completed, an architect asked to see his plans, but he couldn't show them because he didn't have any. God had given him the insight to do it. God gives us the blessing we need at the time we need it. God does not need someone to carry out His desires. He can do it alone. But, as His children, He enjoys working together to accomplish our Father's Will. To do so, we must have an intimate relationship with the Lord to know His Will. The Lord will never force anyone to do His Will. This is our choice. The only thing we have is our *yes* to the Lord. If we can recognize ourselves as nothing without Him and if we recognize that He loves us, then we are walking with God. He wants you happy, and He wants to help you grow. With Jesus, we are victorious. The enemy has already been defeated.

At this point in the book, I do want to clarify something important. I accepted God's Will to write this book to share the truths I discovered in my life to help others. So, it's important for me to give you the full truth. Churches sometimes make mistakes (Catholic and other Christian churches). It could be deliberate or unintentional. Regardless, the wolves are all over and in different levels of society. Jesus said, "See, I am sending you out like sheep into the midst of wolves; so be wise as serpents and innocent as doves." (Matt 10, 16 NRSV). We are among people, and people make mistakes.

On the spiritual side, my advice is if you don't feel comfortable in a church, are faced with something that this inappropriate, or are getting teachings that are not according to the Bible, leave. Don't even hesitate.

It's painful, I know. I still feel the pain of attending Mass on Sundays without knowing about confession and individual confession. The church I was attending when I was young had even removed the confessionals from the church. That doesn't make sense. This is one of the reasons why my soul was dying. If the soul dies, the individual will not survive long either. So, if you're not comfortable and do not feel supported in your faith, it is better to continue your spiritual journey with people in another Christian or Catholic church. It is, in fact, your responsibility to do so. If you are not sure which church to go to, ask God, and

He will show you a better place. Let Him lead the way. Trust Him. The Christian faith is broad and full of marvelous works of the Lord. That is what Pope John Paul II meant when he spoke of ecumenism. It is not a matter of a single faith. It involves all Christian denominations. We need to sort out our differences to move according to God's plan, not our plan.

Catholic priests are available to offer all the sacraments (Baptism, Eucharist, Confirmation, Reconciliation [Confession], Anointing of the Sick, Marriage, and Ordination). If you are not Catholic and would like to be one, there is a course that you would need to follow. It is called the Rite of Christian Initiation of Adults (RCIA). You can simply contact a Catholic church to know if they have this program.

If you are looking for advice, for example, should I get married? Should I change careers? Ask these questions to the Lord; He will guide you. Ask the Holy Spirit to give you dreams or inspiration to understand the Will of God. It is difficult for a priest to answer these types of questions, even if he has the best intentions. Go to Mass. Go to church at least every Sunday. Be faithful to the church you go to. Jesus is already there waiting to listen to you and to help you.

Over the years, the Lord taught me something about confession. This sacrament is so wonderful because we really feel relief after saying our sins to a priest. But what I didn't realize is that we can also offer up the sins of others. There was a priest I knew who did something to me that was completely unthinkable. I never mentioned it to anybody except my husband. I could have pressed criminal charges, but I didn't. I wanted to show mercy toward the priest.

We were just about to celebrate Easter. On Friday, the day of the Passion, it is a tradition to read the passages of the Crucifixion. I cannot tell you how much I felt God's mercy. I was chosen to be the reader of the Crucifixion. The priest had a hard time getting out and doing the celebration. I guess he didn't know what I planned to do while I was going to do the readings.

God gave me the strength to read it all and to stay calm. I was reading the crucifixion, and the priest was replying as Jesus. This was the hardest thing I had to do as an animator. I had read many times before for many different occasions but never in this type of context. I stayed calm, and I united myself with Jesus. This is what God wanted. The Lord wanted to show me that He was bearing our sins. He was carrying them to the Cross. Jesus presented Himself as a sinner to His Father.

I did what I was asked to do, and I never went back to that church. The pain stayed for a few years. During Sunday Mass, I would often cry, and if it wasn't for God's grace, I would have left church and never come back. My conversion helped me to stay strong and to stay firm in my faith. One day, as my family and I were doing Adoration, I started crying. Suddenly, the pain I felt from that situation surfaced. It seemed to have come from nowhere. I felt so bad about what had happened. There was a priest available for confession during that time, so I decided to go. As I was waiting to give this to the Lord, my tears just kept on falling. The pain was so strong. It wasn't my sin, so I never thought of talking about it to a priest. Yet, Jesus wanted me to give it to Him during confession. I had such a hard time talking because the pain was so strong and deep inside me.

After saying this confession, I was relieved. I was very embarrassed about it, but it happened. This showed me that confession is not just for our sins but also for the sins of others. Jesus heals and takes care of the rest. I felt liberated after confession.

So, the church hurt me both spiritually by not offering individual confession when I was young and temporally (physically), but neither was a reason to leave Church. These were not reasons to abandon my faith. Who is without sin? "[. . .] 'Let anyone among you who is without sin be the first to throw a stone at her'" (John 8:7 NRSV). At the end of this story, nobody threw a single rock. If you choose to leave church, you are hurting yourself. Give the hurt to Jesus, even if it's not your fault. He is the one that heals. Make peace for yourself.

If you have read this book from the beginning, we can easily analyze what went wrong in my life. Why was I hurt?

Did I respect God's Commandments? No
What was the source of the problem? Satan
Who put me in temptation and in ignorance? Satan
Who wanted me to leave church to prevent me from being
    protected by God? Satan
Did Jesus die for all our sins to give us life? Yes
Did Jesus give us His name to rebuke the devil? Yes
Did Jesus give us confession to heal us? Yes
Is Jesus the Way, the Truth, and the Life? Yes
Did Jesus give us sacraments to bless us and protect us?
    Yes

Now, let's use the same questions for something you might have read in the newspaper that made you sad or upset that God didn't do anything.

Did someone miss out on God's Commandment? Yes
What was the source of the problem? Satan
Who put the person in temptation? Satan
Who wanted to wreck and kill? Satan

What did Jesus already do for us?
He died for all our sins to give us life because He loves us. By doing so, He gave us His name to rebuke the devil. He gave us sacraments to parallel every step of our lives. He gave us a guardian angel. He gave us confession to heal us. He gives us life even when we are depressed or our soul is dying. Confession helps us not to sin again. If the sin comes back, go back to confession. It will go away. We need Jesus and His teachings. This is what He meant when he said: "For my yoke is easy, and my burden is light." (Matthew 11:30 NRSV). We need to put God in our lives. Not just attending church sometimes or praying sometimes, but

every day. It needs to be part of you. This is how you can build a relationship with God by placing Him first.

Now that you have discernment. What do we do about it?

We can resist evil by praying every day, fasting, attending Mass at least on Sundays, reading the Bible every day, going to Confession (preferably once a month), using Jesus' name every day, and asking the Saints to intercede for you. Some saints have a special area they can help in. For example, St. Antoine is well known to help us find something we may have lost, while St. Blaise is the patron saint for sore throats. St. Peregrine is the patron of cancer patients; you can also pray in tongues every day, sing to the Lord, and praise Him. The Church holds many treasures. These spiritual treasures are all available to us. Humanity needs Jesus. He is our Creator. There is no way around it.

CHAPTER 9

Blessings Received

Before moving to Ontario, I had just completed another degree in Languages. I wanted to specialize in writing. As soon as I finished these studies, my health was not the same. My body had a hard time keeping any liquids. Each time I had an episode, I would go to the hospital to see what was causing the terrible symptoms. I trusted the medical profession to the point where I admired their knowledge compared to my own. Reality brought me to reason. Health professionals were not able to help me. The doctors and the nurses didn't know what was wrong.

My family doctor didn't know what I was going through. The tests didn't reveal anything. Yet, my stomach was sore, and I couldn't retain any fluid. This would happen almost every other day. I was so sick! It would hurt so badly! The medicine I took controlled the symptoms to some extent, but it made me very drowsy. I couldn't have a normal and healthy week. That was quite a shock. My perspective on medical science changed during this ordeal. I didn't have any medical help.

After several months with this horrible disease, a radiologist asked me a few questions. Even though it wasn't part of her role, I could see she wanted to help me. She was the only healthcare worker that was on the right track. She told me to write down what I ate and see what could be making me sick. After doing that for a week, I realized I could barely eat. I prayed for the Lord's help. I still had to take care of my child. I thought surely I was going to die from this mystery ailment.

My stomach was hurting so much. It was a difficult period. We were renovating the house during that time, and there wasn't much peace. I had to clean up after the contractors left, the washrooms had to be renovated, and George was looking after the other house in Quebec. I was basically alone with my son most of the time and sick.

My parents came to see us on a Sunday. When they were about to leave, I looked at my mother, hinting that I didn't have much time to live. She tried to find solutions online. She found a Specific Carbohydrate Diet. I had to answer several questions online. Once I finished the quiz, it was recommended that I take their course. I don't believe everything there is on the Internet, but, in my situation, I felt I didn't have anything to lose. I enrolled in the class. I had all kinds of doubts regarding it. I had to follow different steps: what to eat, how to cook the food, and what to avoid eating. There was a lot of cooking at the beginning, but from one week to the next, I was improving. My symptoms became much more manageable. They recommended reading a book called *Breaking the Vicious Cycle: Intestinal Health Through Diet* by Elaine Gloria Gottschall. The course and this book were both extremely useful and helpful. I thanked the Lord and my mother for their help and guidance.

However, that wasn't the end of the story. Jesus came to my aid once more. During homeschooling, I would sometimes go on the Internet to look at different documentaries with my son. On the side of the screen, he found a link that spoke of different spiritual topics. I didn't know the program well, so I didn't trust it. Regardless, I decided to give it a chance, and I jumped halfway through the episode. Since it made sense, we listened to it. From this program, I was led to a spiritual testimony. It was Kevin Zadai's testimony. In the end, he prayed for someone who was suffering from digestive problems. As soon as he mentioned this, I sensed warmth all along my digestive tract. Jesus healed me! I continued the SCD diet for two weeks. Then I decided to eat a cookie that wasn't made with the recommended SCD food. After eating it, I wasn't sick. Thank you, Lord! Jesus healed me of this terrible illness that couldn't be diagnosed. I follow a hypotoxic diet. This is not due to any symptoms but because it is a lot healthier. By following SCD, I realized how important it is to eat well and how much food can affect our bodies.

After going through all this, the blessings received were enormous. I discovered how to pray in Jesus' name, asking for people's healing thanks to a course offered at Dr. Zadai's school of ministry: Warrior Notes. After going through such a difficult period, Jesus gave me the motivation and compassion to help others. Jesus wants us to go and heal the sick just like He did.

Each one of us has a unique role in helping our brothers and sisters. Saint Paul explains, "The gifts he gave were that some would be apostles, some prophets, some evangelists, some pastors and teachers, to equip the saints for the work of ministry, for building up the body of Christ, [. . .]" (Ephesians 4:11-12 NSRV). We all have our jobs to do within the body of Christ.

CHAPTER 10

Unexpected Illness

In May 2021, George became ill and suffered from headaches. He would have pain all day. It had never happened to him before. For fourteen years, we always said the Rosary together without any issues. But when George's illness started, he was confused and even forgot some words. I would give him basic medication to ease the pain, but it would always come back. Because he seemed to be forgetful, I thought it was Alzheimer's disease.

His illness was worsening day by day. At the end of the week, George could hardly stand up to walk. One morning, we finished saying our prayers, and then he stood up from his chair. It's a good thing I was next to him because he started to fall. I grabbed him by the waist. Our son ran to get George a cane to get his balance. It seemed his health was declining more and more every day. I didn't want to acknowledge it. My parents, who dropped by, strongly suggested calling an ambulance. There was no choice. I had to call 911. He was sent to a hospital. From there, he was transferred to two more hospitals. I kept getting calls in the middle of the night from nurses and doctors, letting me know where he was and which tests were being done. The next morning, a surgeon called, telling me they found a brain tumor. George needed an operation.

They removed the tumor and tested it to know what it was. He had a glioblastoma. This meant he only had a few months to live. The operation was successful, but in only a few weeks, the tumor was already growing back rapidly. During that time, we had an appointment at the cancer clinic to talk to the doctors who could treat this type of cancer. They offered ways to reduce the growth of the tumor. They showed us the size of the tumor before it was removed. It was taking up almost half of his brain. I wanted to respect George's decision since he had to go through all this. After a few days, George decided he wanted to surrender to God's Will. He knew the treatments would be hard and the quality of life would be worse. It was hard to accept, but I understood. The treatments were not easy, and he was very weak.

George wanted to go home. He didn't want to eat at the hospital. He kept saying he wanted to eat at home. A nurse called me in to make sure he would eat. That meant driving two hours each day to be by his side. After a few days, they moved him to a closer hospital. It was still strongly recommended that he stayed in the hospital for a few more weeks.

However, when I came into the hospital, a nurse said that they were thinking of releasing him right away. I didn't agree with that since the surgeon said to keep him for at least two more weeks. George was losing patience. He couldn't sleep in the previous hospital, and the hospital he was in wasn't better. The doctor released him within a few hours, saying to me, "We can't blame the guy for wanting to go home." I was shocked! Is that science? How could I take care of him? He just had brain surgery! They gave me a long list of medications to get for him, and I tried to set up the house as functionally as I could to make things easy for him.

I served him a good meal as soon as he arrived. I was happy to see that he ate a lot, but he didn't have a lot of energy. He could only look at the television and sleep. After watching an episode, he decided to lie down. I could see that he was sad. I tried to encourage him. I wanted to bring spiritual encouragement by saying to look at the future, meaning Jesus and heaven. When he woke up, I was working in the kitchen. I had to go to the basement for a few minutes. Suddenly, I heard a kitchen drawer open. I found that strange. I went back upstairs, and to my surprise, George was in the kitchen. He was holding something behind his back. I could hear something clinging. I asked him "What is that sound?" He showed me three knives, the three longest ones we used in the kitchen. Without giving it a second thought, I looked him in the eyes, saying, "You don't need that." He put them back in the drawer. Thank you, Lord!

I asked him if he wanted to take fresh air outside. He always liked the outdoors and agreed. As we were going towards the deck through the garage, he looked at the saws that were hanging on a panel. I didn't like the way he eyed them intensely as we were walking by. I let him go on the deck, and I locked the door behind him.

During that time, I unhooked each saw as fast as I could, and I hid them in the basement. I removed everything harmful I could see. George wasn't happy with me, and he was knocking on the door. I opened the door as quickly as I could, and he told me he didn't want me to do that again. I agreed and brought him back inside the house. George watched more television. During that time, I talked to my son and warned him that it was very important to lock his door before going to bed. When bedtime came, I heard him lock his door. I was relieved, but I slept uneasily during the night. I wasn't sure what was to come, but I gave everything to God. The suffering was unbearable. I surrendered to God. I trusted Him. My son's future and mine were in God's hands.

The next day was Father's Day. I was hopeful that this would help George. When the morning came, I explained to George that we were going to use the day to celebrate him. I was very happy on that special day, but he seemed upset. He was disappointed that he continued to have trouble sleeping even though he was at home. He had also been diagnosed with lung cancer, so I had left the fan on for him, but that didn't seem to help. I could see he was losing patience.

He wanted pills. I didn't know what to give him. There were so many pills to choose from. Some were strong; others were milder. He suggested that I should go to the pharmacy and ask for different pills. As soon as my parents came in, I warned them about George's depression resurfacing. My father accompanied me to the pharmacy. I left my mother and my son with George. That was very stressful.

During that time, the pharmacist explained that the pills take at least a week or two before taking effect. George and I knew that was true because of the other depressions he had. When we returned from the pharmacy, I gave him what I thought would be best, considering what was already prescribed and the pharmacist's explanations.

My mother prepared a nice meal for us, and we all ate except for George. He was very quiet. Afterwards, we thought it would be a good idea to sit outside on the deck. My mother suggested that I lie down to rest for a little while. I agreed.

While I was trying to rest, something told me to make a photocopy of the pills George was taking during his depression. We had a doctor's appointment the next day, and I wanted to see what he could suggest. While I was making a photocopy, my mother screamed in the house that George had gone into the pool and was trying to commit suicide. He had found a hammer in the garage. I ran to the phone to call 911. My son looked for a rope for my parents to keep George's head above water. They were able to keep him under control with his cane and the rope. I couldn't believe what was happening. I was thinking of all the saws I hid, but I never considered the hammers in the drawer.

I was screaming on the phone. The lady was trying to keep me calm. I was shaking like a leaf. How could he have done this on Father's Day? We had wanted to celebrate him. His disease always seemed to make him think the opposite way.

The ambulance came while my parents were still keeping George's head above water. They saved his life. While the paramedics were placing him on a stretcher, I couldn't look at him. I was so disappointed. He went to the hospital while I had to face so many questions. I had to explain everything to the police, paramedics, nurses, doctors, psychologists, and even palliative care. There was one phone call after another. Each time, this terrible scene came alive.

It took at least three weeks before I could tolerate seeing George. I was very mad at him. I had a hard time accepting what he had done in front of his own child and in front of my parents. He wasn't thinking right for sure; it was so hard to accept. We always prayed for life. Life should be respected. We firmly believed that. I tried to change my anger to understanding. I am sure God opened my heart at that point. I tried to think about the operation and the size of the tumor. While I was thinking about that, I also thought of someone who shared his painful journey with his wife when she passed away. He said that his goal was to bring her to the gates of Heaven. I found that mission so beautiful. I wanted to live by that. I wanted to be with George even if it wasn't going to be easy to face him. These thoughts gave me courage. I wanted to bring George to the gates of Heaven.

I also wanted to live according to Saint Paul's explanation about love found in 1 Corinthians 13. With this in mind, I focused on Jesus' cross. I gave all my sufferings to God. I went to see George at the hospital with a very heavy heart. When I arrived at his room, there was a security guard at the door. He didn't look well. We didn't talk about what he had done. There was really nothing to say. I just tried to do what I could to make him comfortable.

I tried to be as merciful as I could possibly be. Many months later, during a homily, I discovered that it was a ministry by itself: the ministry of God's presence.

While I was at the hospital that day, I had to meet the medical team taking care of George. They gave me different options to help him. One of which surprised me a lot! George had requested euthanasia. How could that be? We had prayed together for so many years. We believe strongly that life is worth protecting. Catholics are pro-life. This means they want to preserve life from conception to death. I just couldn't understand how his thinking had become contrary to his convictions. It wasn't him anymore. I now had to fight for his life in another way. I had to save his soul.

Fortunately, I had the support of our priest, who contacted the bishop regarding this matter. Our legal documents were in order, so this gave me an additional chance to protect him from his own decisions. In addition, his medical condition didn't give him the capacity to think about this clearly. God allowed me the chance to save his soul. Thank you, Lord! I contacted the chaplain at the hospital. I was relieved to learn that George was able to have confession and The Sacrament of Anointing of the Sick.

I kept on seeing him every week. My son eventually had permission to see his father. It was a difficult area since he was in a psychiatric ward, and the COVID restrictions made it very difficult. We tried to make it as enjoyable as we could. George kept on giving me his personal belongings. I didn't want to take them, but we both knew what was coming.

George wanted to come back home. After what had previously happened, I couldn't even think about that. The psychiatrists seemed to agree with the idea of George coming home, and I was shocked! How could they think that? How can everything be fine after such a tragic event at home? They determined he was stable and could go home as long as he took his medication. I couldn't even imagine living in fear again! I couldn't go down that road again. I strongly disagreed with them. At that point, I had to put my foot down.

Many nurses and specialists surrounded me. With conviction, I said that I would make the hospital personally responsible for that decision if they chose to discharge him; I had a son to protect, and George wasn't thinking clearly. How could I predict what he was thinking and prevent something terrible from happening? His depression was still there. The conversations between George and me were not reassuring during my visits. The "specialists" didn't have that information.

I tried to find another option for George. I needed a room in a long-term care facility. The health system didn't make my situation easy. With God's help, though, I was able to find a residence. On the day of the transfer, George lost his orientation. The hospital decided to keep him as a palliative patient. His speech wasn't as clear, and he was repeating himself. From week to week, we could see that his health was going down. My son and I played the song "Ave Maria" in Armenian. I had heard that this specific song heals tumors. We kept on hoping for him to be healed. A Christian never loses hope!

One day, we received encouraging news. A nurse called to say that they would change his diet and give him more consistent meals since he was getting better. My son and I were very happy. His birthday was coming up, and we were really looking forward to celebrating it with him. We had everything prepared to go the next morning.

At 9 p.m., the telephone rang. Another nurse called to inform me that George had passed away. My family and I went to the hospital as fast as we could to say our last goodbye. How sad this was for all of us! Six months after the surgery, George died a few hours before his 70th birthday. My son and I couldn't believe it. We were preparing to celebrate his last birthday together, but it wasn't possible. We left his room, and the only words that came up were, "He's resting now." The nurses and my parents stood around me to show their support. All I could do was cry.

Three days after George passed away, I wasn't feeling well, and I was very sad. I woke up that morning, and I sensed God asking me what I would do if I saw George again. I replied in my heart that "I would give him such a big hug!" Then I cried. I felt God answering me by saying, "You are tired; continue sleeping." I went back to bed and fell asleep. While sleeping, I had a dream. I saw George in a waiting room. He was right next to a door, and I was in front of him. That was my chance; I gave him such a great big hug and then looked at him. His eyes were closed; he smiled. In his ear, God made me ask him a question. The words that came out of my mouth were so clear. It had everything to do with life! The blessings I have received since then have been nothing but incredible and miraculous. I hope to share them with you in person.

We must always keep this in mind. After Jesus' Crucifixion, there was life. Jesus was resurrected. Power and glory came out of these difficult moments. God's power empties graves! Jesus came back with the keys to Heaven and Hell. Jesus gave us His name. Jesus frees us from sin if we repent. He is Almighty and empowers us when we trust in Him.

The Bible says, "But he said to me, 'My grace is sufficient for you, for power is made perfect in weakness.' So, I will boast all the more gladly about my weaknesses, so that the power of Christ may dwell in me" (2 Corinthian 12:9, NRSV). We must make the effort to make the right decisions according to Jesus' teachings.

Do you remember when the Apostles were in the boat with Jesus, and a big storm started? It was getting so bad that the Apostles thought surely the boat would sink. Now, think of this. Who was in the boat with them? It was Jesus, the Man-God, Christ Himself. The Creator. Why were they afraid? It's because they didn't really realize Who was with them. If they really had known that the Creator was with them, they wouldn't have feared. Our lives are just like being on that boat with Jesus. Do we need to fear? No, He is waiting for us to ask for His help. He is a step ahead of us.

Somehow our human will makes us stray from the narrow path. We neglect to seek the Word of God. We feel we can find truths in new philosophies, visions, ways of well-being, or super-hero characters. When all along, Jesus is our hero. Jesus has all the answers. Jesus is our comfort. Jesus brings peace to our lives. He brings His peace. Jesus is the One Who can help us. We do not need to look further. He loves you the way you are, and He will never abandon you. Never! "'[. . .]Lord, show us the Father and we will be satisfied.' Jesus said to him, 'Have I been with you all this time, Philip, and you still do not know me? Whoever has seen me has seen the Father [. . .]" (John 14:8–9 NRSV).

Conclusion

I just want to clarify that the goal of this book is not to make you a Catholic. If I have shared more about this faith, it is because this is the faith I practice and grew up in. I am not by any means forcing anybody to change their Christian faith. I am simply sharing what I lived to help you walk with Jesus in your life. I have seen and lived signs and wonders in both the Catholic faith and the Christian faith. This proves to me that God is active in both. It is through these churches that we can have a beautiful intimacy with Jesus by protecting ourselves from evil. This book comes from my heart to yours to help you where you are right now. This book is not funded by any religious groups. I wrote it because Jesus asked me to share my testimony, plain and simple. I lost a lot of time searching. I truly hope this book helped you. I know one thing. If you say yes to Jesus, He will be able to protect you, guide you, and give you what you need. Dear readers, you are all in my prayers.

Going back to the beginning of this book, I understand a little more about the teacher who was asking the students to make a line. I am still in that line, but the Master's voice is clearer now. The purpose of life is more specific. Live to love and give glory to God. That is my passion and our mission. That is the life of God's children to their Creator. Only God can make us happy. It is up to us to say yes to Him and trust Him in total surrender to be happy for eternity. There is always good that comes out of bad experiences. We do not need to fear. Jesus won the battle for us. Jesus can help. He has plenty of blessings to give to all His children. It is up to us to walk alongside Jesus and to fully trust in Him. He is waiting for your *yes*. Are you ready to give it to Him? In April 2022, Pope Francis said during the Easter homily "Brothers and sisters our hope has a name: the name of Jesus". (Hattrup, 2022)

God's Ten Commandments

The Bible mentions the Ten Commandments twice. Once in Exodus and once more in Deuteronomy.

Exodus 20: 1–17 NRSV

"Then God spoke all these words: I am the Lord your God, who brought you out of the land of Egypt, out of the house of slavery; you shall have no other gods before me. You shall not make for yourself an idol, whether in the form of anything that is in heaven above, or that is on the earth beneath, or that is in the water under the earth. You shall not bow down to them or worship them; for I the Lord your God am a jealous God, punishing children for the iniquity of parents, to the third and fourth generation of those who reject me, but showing steadfast love to the thousandth generation of those who love me and keep my commandments. You shall not make wrongful use of the name of the Lord your God, for the Lord will not acquit anyone who misuses his name. Remember the sabbath day, and keep it holy. Six days you shall labour and do all your work. But the seventh day is a sabbath to the Lord your God; you shall not do any work – you, your son or your daughter, your male or female slave, your livestock, or the alien resident in your towns. For in six days the Lord made heaven and earth, the sea, and all that is in them, but rested the seventh day; therefore the Lord blessed the sabbath day and consecrated it. Honour your father and your mother, so that your days may be long in the land that the Lord your God is giving you. You shall not murder. You shall not commit adultery. You shall not steal. You shall not bear false witness against your neighbour.

You shall not covet your neighbour's house; you shall not covet your neighbour's wife, or male or female slave, or ox, or donkey, or anything that belongs to your neighbour."

Deuteronomy 5:6–21 NRSV
"I am the Lord your God, who brought you out of the land of Egypt, out of the house of slavery; you shall have no other gods before me. You shall not make for yourself an idol, whether in the form of anything that is in heaven above, or that is on the earth beneath, or that is in the water under the earth. You shall not bow down to them or worship them; for I the Lord your God am a jealous God, punishing children for the iniquity of parents, to the third and fourth generation of those who reject me, but showing steadfast love to the thousandth generation of those who love me and keep my commandments. You shall not make wrongful use of the name of the Lord your God, for the Lord will not acquit anyone who misuses his name. Observe the sabbath day and keep it holy, as the Lord your God commanded you. Six days you shall labour and do all your work. But the seventh day is a sabbath to the Lord your God; you shall not do any work -you, or your son or your daughter, or your male or female slave, or your ox or your donkey, or any of your livestock, or the resident alien in your towns, so that your male and female slave may rest as well as you. Remember that you were a slave in the land of Egypt, and the Lord your God brought you out from there with a mighty hand and an outstretched arm; therefore the Lord your God commanded you to keep the sabbath day. Honour your father and your mother, as the Lord your God commanded you, so that your days may be long and that it may go well with you in the land that the Lord your God is giving you. You shall not murder." Neither shall you commit adultery. Neither shall you steal. Neither shall you bear false witness against your neighbour. Neither shall you covet your neighbor's wife. Neither shall you desire your neighbour's house, or field, or male or female slave, or ox, or donkey, or anything that belongs to your neighbour."

Bibliography

Carothers, M. (1972). *Power in praise* (1st ed.). Escondido, CA: M.R. Carothers.

Doucette, Fr. Melvin. (2007).*Staple Bound*, Privately Published, Tignish, P.E.I.

Gottschall, Elaine (2020). *Breaking the Vicious Cycle: Intestinal Health Through Diet*. The Kirkton Press.

Holy Bible NRSV, The British and Foreign Bible Society, (2012). Bible Society Resources Ltd.

Hattrup, K. N. (2022, April 16). *Pope: Our hope has a name! full text of Easter Vigil homily* Retrieved January 29, 2023, from https://aleteia.org/2022/04/16/pope-our-hope-has-a-name-full-text-of-easter-vigil-homily/

Kelley, B. (2012). *The New Saint Joseph Baltimore Catechism* (1st ed.). New Jersey: Catholic Book Publishing Corp.

Lachance, L. (1999). *For the happiness of my own, my chosen ones, Jesus.* Sherbrooke, QC: St. Raphael Publications.

Paul, J. (2006). *Catechism of the Catholic Church* (1st ed.). Ottawa: Canadian Conference of Catholic Bishops.

Pontifical Council For Culture, Pontifical Council For Interreligious Dialogue, Jesus Christ The Bearer of the Water of Life, *A Christian reflection on the "New Age."* Vatican. Retrieved January 30, 2023, from https://www.vatican.va/roman_curia/pontifical_councils/interelg/documents/rc_pc_interelg_doc_20030203_new-age_en.html

John Paul II (1981, November 22). *Familiaris Consortio, The Role of the Christian Family in the Modern World.* Retrieved January 30, 2023, from https://www.vatican.va/content/john-paul-ii/en/apost_exhortations/documents/hf_jp-ii_exh_19811122_familiaris-consortio.html

Reasoners, Jordan, Steve Wright. (2009). *SCD Lifestyle Surviving to Thriving.* SFK, LLC.

Strong, J., & Baker, W. (2004). *Strong's complete word study concordance* (1st ed.). Chattanooga, Tenn.: AMG Publishers.

Valtorta, M., Picozzi, N., & McLaughlin, P. (1986). *Poem of the Man God Volume 1.* CENTRO EDITORIALE VALTORTIANO.

Noonan, M. (Speaker). (2012). *Vatican Teaching on the New Age* [DVD]. Ave Maria Centre of Peace.

Sid Roth. (2016, December 4). *Kevin Zadai Died. What Jesus Showed Him Will Amaze You!* [Video]. YouTube. https://www.youtube.com/watch?v=b7m3pOdINno

Zadai, K. (n.d.). *Warrior Notes School of Ministry*. Warrior Notes. Retrieved January 30, 2023, from https://www.warriornotesschool.com/

Special Thanks

I would like to thank God for His love toward all His children. Thank you for Your mercy, Your teachings, Your guidance, Your patience, and Your constant protection. May I always be a humble servant in Your hands. Thank you, Lord, for Your Love.

Thank you to my parents and family. Their faithfulness, advice, mercy, courage, help, and support have been exemplary. Thank you for your love.

Thank you to my son for his patience, help, courage, and determination. Your support and understanding mean a lot to me. Thank you for your love.

Thank you to all the people I met along my path. I was able to grow spiritually due to the different circumstances God placed us in. Thank you for your love.

Disclaimer

All the names have been changed to protect the confidentiality of the people involved.

The health recommendations in this book need to be confirmed by your medical doctor and/or specialist(s) if you decide to follow them. The advice published in the book *Jesus in My Life* is not intended to replace the services of a medical doctor. It is at the reader's discretion to follow the information provided. The author is not liable for any direct or indirect claim, loss, or damage resulting from the information contained in the book *Jesus in My Life* and whatever could be linked to and/or from it.

www.ingramcontent.com/pod-product-compliance
Lightning Source LLC
Chambersburg PA
CBHW071100090426
42737CB00013B/2409